Student Almanac of Native American History

Volume 1: From Prehistoric Times

to the Trail of Tears,

35,000 BCE–1838

Student Almanac of Native American History

Volume 1: From Prehistoric Times

to the Trail of Tears,

35,000 BCE–1838

GREENWOOD PRESS
Westport, Connecticut • London

Library of Congress Cataloging-in-Publication Data
Media Projects, Inc.
Student almanac of Native American history.
      p. cm.—(Middle school reference)
  Includes bibliographical references and index.
  ISBN 0–313–32599–5 (set: alk. paper)—ISBN 0–313–32600–2 (v. 1: alk. paper)—
ISBN 0–313–32601–0 (v. 2: alk. paper)
  1. Indians of North America—History. [1. Indians of North America—History.] I. Series.
E77.S925 2003
970'.00497—dc21   2002035215

British Library Cataloguing in Publication Data is available.

Library of Congress Catalog Card Number: 2002035215
ISBN: 0–313–32599–5 (set)
        0–313–32600–2 (vol. 1)
        0–313–32601–0 (vol. 2)

First published in 2003

Greenwood Press, 88 Post Road West, Westport, CT 06881
An imprint of Greenwood Publishing Group, Inc.
www.greenwood.com

Printed in the United States of America

The paper used in this book complies with the
Permanent Paper Standard issued by the National
Information Standards Organization (Z39.48–1984).

10 9 8 7 6 5 4 3 2 1

A Media Projects, Inc. Production
Contributing Writers: George Ochoa, Melinda Corey,
Elin Woodger, Norman Murphy, Michele Camardella, Doreen Russo
Design: Amy Henderson
Production: Anthony Galante and Jim Burmester
Editor: Carter Smith
Indexer: Marilyn Flaig

CONTENTS

Volume 1: From Prehistoric Times to the Trail of Tears, 35,000 BCE–1838

From Prehistoric Times to the Trail of Tears

35,000 BCE–1838

"Shall we give up our homes, our country, bequeathed to us by the Great Spirit, the graves of our dead, and everything that is dear and sacred to us, without a struggle? I know you will cry with me: Never! Never!"

—Tecumseh, Shawnee chief, 1811

Native American history began when the first people crossed into the Americas at least 35,000 years ago. But most of the history that we now know took place after 1492, when Europeans first arrived in the Americas. It was in that part of their history that Native Americans suffered their greatest tragedy. What took place led to the deaths of many of their people. It also almost destroyed their way of life — the way that Native Americans had been living for thousands of years.

This first volume of *Student Almanac of Native American History* looks at the many peoples that made up Native America and how and where they lived. It also describes what happened once explorers and settlers from Europe first came to America and some of what happened in the years that followed.

THE EARLIEST IMMIGRANTS

This book tells the early history of Native Americans in three main parts. The first part, found in Chapter 1, discusses how Native Americans first came to the Americas. It also describes how the earliest Native Americans roamed from place to place, hunting large animals that are now extinct, such as woolly mammoths and saber-toothed tigers.

As these large animals began to die out, some tribes stopped hunting and started planting crops like corn and building permanent villages instead of moving from place to place. Especially in Mexico and South America, some of these permanent settlements grew to become large cities that were homes to powerful empires. Some of these empires include the **Maya** (see p. 37) and **Aztec** (see p. 24) of Mexico and the **Inca** (see p. 34) of Peru.

Hundreds of other Native American civilizations lived north of Mexico, in what are now the United States and Canada. Some of the oldest of these, such as the **Anasazi** (see p. 21) of the Southwest or the **Mound Builders** (see p. 39) of the Southeast and Midwest, built large cities, where they lived off crops they grew. Other peoples settled in smaller villages, where they also grew crops or fished from nearby riverbanks. Still others, especially on the Great Plains that stretch from the Mississippi River to the Rocky Mountains, continued to move from place to place hunting for their food. Rather than tracking woolly mammoths as their ancestors had, they hunted a new source of food—the buffalo.

THE EUROPEANS ARRIVE

Chapter 2 of *Student Almanac of Native American History* describes what happened when the first European explorers arrived in the Americas, or what they called "The New World." It describes who the different groups of Europeans were and how they reacted to the Native Americans they found here. Some of the stories are famous, such as the story of **Pocahontas** (see p. 79) and the English settlers who settled at Jamestown, Virginia. Some stories are not. But no matter which country they came from, many of the Europeans had one thing in common. They were more interested in what the other European countries were doing there than in sharing the land with the Native Americans that had been there before them all.

Christopher Columbus arrives in the New World. (Library of Congress)

The years between 1492—when **Christopher Columbus** arrived (see p. 60)—and 1763—when Great Britain forced France out of most of the Americas—were a time when European countries fought for control of the Americas. In North America, this was especially true in what is now the eastern half of the United States and Canada. It was in this part of the Americas that France and Great Britain had most of their American colonies. In order to survive, many Native American peoples were forced to pick sides in a series of wars known as the **French and Indian Wars** (see p. 62), by allying themselves with either of these two European nations.

During the three centuries that followed Columbus's arrival, not all Europeans treated Native Americans badly. Native Americans learned many useful things from the Europeans, such as how to use horses, build wheels, and make metal tools. For the most part, though, Indians suffered greatly from contact with the new settlers. Many thousands were killed in battles, while even more died from diseases that the Europeans brought with them.

Chapter 2 comes to an end just before the **American Revolution** (see p. 99) took place and the United States was born. After the United States won its independence from Great Britain, Native Americans would continue to pay a terrible price.

NATIVE AMERICANS AND THE EARLY UNITED STATES

After the American Revolution, the new United States stretched all the way from the Atlantic Ocean in the east to the Mississippi River in the west. Even though most Americans still lived within 50 miles of the Atlantic coastline, many of them started looking west for new land that seemed to be theirs for the taking.

The final chapter of this volume of the *Student Almanac of Native American History* tells about what happened to the Native Americans in the eastern United States as American settlers moved westward toward the Mississippi River onto their land. Often, what happened involved violence. During the early years of U.S. history that are covered in this chapter, Americans and Indians fought many wars over land. Among these were **Little Turtle's War** (1790–1795) (see p. 112), **Tecumseh's Rebellion** (1809–1813) (see p. 118), and the **Black Hawk War** (1832) (see p. 101). With each war, Native Americans lost more more land to white settlers from the United States.

The United States did not stop growing when it reached the Mississippi River, of course. This chapter also discusses how the United States gained even more new territory. First, in 1803, France sold almost all of the rest of its land in North America to the United States. This sale, called the Louisiana Purchase, doubled the size of the United States. Then, in 1819, the United States grew again when it purchased Florida from Spain.

With each of these land purchases, more and more land inhabited by Native American peoples was claimed by the United States. White settlers flowed into those lands and new wars started. Native Americans won some battles, but in the end the expansion of the United States was unstoppable. By the 1830s, almost all the Native Americans in the eastern

United States were forced to move west. One such people, the **Cherokee**, (see p. 25) were forced to move from their homes in the Southeast to Oklahoma in 1838–1839, in what became known as the **Trail of Tears** (see p. 121).

After that, the struggle between the United States and Native Americans moved west, where the fighting continued throughout most of the 19th century. That part of Native American history, and the story of how Native Americans struggled to keep their traditions and beliefs alive through the 20th century, is included in Volume 2.

HOW TO USE THIS BOOK

Each chapter in *Student Almanac of Native American History* is divided into two parts. The first part is a short essay that gives a summary of the major events in that time in Native American history. The second part is an A-Z section that describes many important people, events, and terms that have to do with the time period.

To help readers find related ideas more easily, many terms are cross-indexed. Within both the essay and A-Z section of each chapter, some words appear in **bold letters**. That means that the term is also a separate A-Z entry in *Student Almanac of Native American History*, which should be read for more information. Other unfamiliar words are printed in ***bold italics***. Short definitions of these words can be found in a glossary on page 127. Finally, words that may be hard to pronounce are followed by a pronunciation key.

Nations of Native America

Before European explorers arrived to stay in North America, hundreds of Native American nations already lived here. They spoke many languages, lived in many different climates, and lived many different ways of life from each other. The map below shows just some of those nations.

CHAPTER ONE

Before Contact

Native American History before Columbus, 35,000 BCE–1491

"There was a time when our people covered the land as the waves of a wind-ruffled sea cover its shell-paved floor."

—Seattle (Sealth), Duwamish-Suquamish chief, 1855

According to their legends, Native Americans are the "First People." They did not travel from anywhere else to get to North America. Instead, they believe they sprang up in America, with help from their gods or spirits. Today, Native Americans value these stories as an important part of their heritage and dismiss scientists and historians who argue that Native Americans did not originate in America.

Although most scholars believe that the first humans in the Americas, meaning North America, Mexico, Central America, and South America, came from somewhere else, they do not agree about when, how, and from where these people came. There are several theories. They all suggest that "Native Americans" *migrated* to the Americas. One popular theory is that during a period called the Ice Age, people migrated from Siberia in northeast Asia across the Bering Strait on a frozen land bridge called *Beringia*. Another is that early voyagers may have come by boat from across the Pacific Ocean. A third theory is that some may have come in wooden canoes across the Bering Strait after the land bridge was underwater. Yet another suggests that some may have even come across the Atlantic Ocean from Europe. These theories present the idea that the Americas were populated over a long period of time and from a variety of different civilizations.

Many historians believe Native Americans first crossed the Bering Strait to reach North America from Asia.

The earliest ancestors of today's Native Americans may have come about 35,000 years ago. That date is supported by studies done by archeologists. Others believe, however, that earlier migrations may have occurred. Once people began to migrate across the continents, they settled into almost every corner of the Americas. Over 12,000 years ago, humans were already living near Monte Verde, Chile, at the far southern tip of South America.

Native American prehistory, the period before written records, can be divided into periods of time. These periods are known as the *Paleolithic* (*pay-lee-oh-LITH-ic*), *Archaic* (*ahr-KAY-ic*), and *Postarchaic* (*post-ahr-KAY-ic*) periods.

THE PALEOLITHIC PERIOD

The people of the Paleolithic period (35,000–9000 BCE) are called Paleo-Indians. They lived by hunting large mammals that are now extinct, such as woolly mammoths, mastodons, saber-toothed tigers, giant sloths, giant beavers, and bighorn bison. They were *nomads*, which means that they followed herds of animals rather than settling in one place. They wore animal hides, lived in caves

Timeline

35,000 BCE   30,000 BCE

The ancestors of Native Americans begin to migrate to the Americas. They probably follow herds of big game animals from Asia across Beringia, the land bridge between Siberia and Alaska.

In the Paleolithic period, which lasts from 30,000 BCE to 9000 BCE, Paleo-Indians hunt mastodons, woolly mammoths, and other large mammals with stone weapons.

or *lean-tos*, and hunted using spears tipped with stone points. Many of these stone points have been found and studied. The differences among them help explain differences among peoples that used them. A spearhead made in about 9500 BCE was found near Clovis, New Mexico. We refer to the people who made this spear as the **Clovis culture** (see p. 27).

Spearheads, propelled by bow and arrow, were among the first hunting and fighting tools used by Native Americans. Blunt spearheads were used for stunning the target and sharp, smooth spearheads were used for hunting since they could easily be removed. Sharp, rough spearheads were used in battle. (Smithsonian Institution)

THE ARCHAIC PERIOD

In the Archaic period (9000–1000 BCE), the large animals of North and South America became extinct. They may have died out from overhunting by humans or from *disease*. As a result, Native Americans started hunting and trapping small game such as deer and fishing and gathering wild plants. In this period, different cultures and customs, or ways of life, began to appear. Among them, the most important was agriculture. In Mexico in about 7000 BCE, pumpkins, gourds, and peppers began to be grown. In Peru, by 6000 BCE, lima beans were grown.

By 5000 BCE, the big game animals were gone. Native American groups found even more food sources, depending on where they lived. In what are

10,000 BCE	9500 BCE	9000 BCE	8000 BCE
Paleo-Indians spread through the Americas as far south as Monte Verde, Chile.	The **Clovis culture**, marked by distinctively fluted spearheads, spreads throughout North America between 9500 BCE and 8000 BCE.	In the Archaic period (9000–1000 BCE), large animals become extinct, possibly from disease or overhunting.	The last Ice Age ends. Melting glaciers raise sea levels, flooding Beringia and creating the Bering Strait.

now the South American countries of Peru and Ecuador, for example, agriculture became a way of life. People there planted beans, squash, and potatoes. By about 4000 BCE, people in Mexico began planting a new crop called *maize* (*MAYZ*), which we call corn. Maize became a very important crop for people in Mesoamerica, the region that stretches from central Mexico to upper Central America. Maize cultivation soon spread to other parts of North America, including what is now the southwestern United States.

As more people settled down to farm, permanent villages and even cities arose. Since people could spend less time looking for food, they had more time to spend constructing permanent homes and other buildings. In Mexico, by about 3000 BCE, people began making huge buildings of stone. Permanent settlements also allowed people to spend time craft-making. In South America, people began making pottery for the first time. They also started making cloth out of cotton and kept llamas and guinea pigs as pets.

THE POSTARCHAIC PERIOD

The Postarchaic period (1500 BCE–1500) was the period in North America before the first Europeans arrived. During this time, agriculture and villages spread. As the number of villages grew, trade between peoples became more common. *Archeologists* have found artifacts, objects made by humans, from this time period in places far from where they were made.

7000 BCE	7000 BCE	5000 BCE	4000 BCE
Big game animals, such as woolly mammoths and mastodons begin to die off by this time. By 5000 BCE, most will be gone.	Agriculture appears in the Americas. In Mexico, farmers are growing pumpkins, gourds, and peppers.	In South America, people of present-day Peru and Ecuador are farming beans, squash, and potatoes.	Maize, or corn, is being cultivated in Mexico. The crop gradually spreads to many parts of the Americas.

A series of amazing cultures developed during this period. The best known of these were called the **Maya** *(MY-uh)* (see p. 37) of Mexico and Central America, the **Aztec** *(AZ-tek)* (see p. 24) of Mexico, and the **Inca** *(IN-cuh)* (see p. 34) of the Andes Mountains in South America. These peoples formed empires with huge cities and towns. They built pyramids, made sculptures, used writing, worked with metal, and studied astronomy and mathematics.

Change was happening everywhere in the Americas in the Postarchaic period. Between 1800 BCE and the 17th century, cultures known as the **Mound Builders** (see p. 39) were at work in North America. The Mound Builders lived throughout the large region from the Great Lakes to the Gulf of Mexico. These people were named after the large mounds of earth they built. These mounds sometimes formed the shapes of animals or geometric figures.

In the Southwest, the people known as the **Anasazi** *(ah-nuh-SAH-zee)* (see p. 21) thrived from about 100 BCE to 1300. For a while, they lived in buildings with many floors and rooms, called *pueblos (PWEB-los)*, on *mesas* or in canyons. Later, they built homes in the sides of cliffs, using ladders to reach them. No one knows for sure why the Anasazi moved into their cliff homes, but many historians believe they moved to protect themselves from attackers.

MANY PEOPLES, MANY LANDS

By 1492, there were as many as 70 to 90 million people in the Americas. These people lived in many hundreds of different Native American groups.

4000 BCE	3000 BCE	2600 BCE	2000 BCE
Ancestors of the Aleut and **Inuit** peoples begin to settle in Alaska.	In central Mexico, settlers construct huge buildings made of stone.	By this time, people are living in large settlements in what is now the southeast U.S. They practice fishing and they trade over long distances.	Ancestors of the **Inuit** settle as far east in the Arctic as Greenland.

They spoke hundreds of different languages. They lived in different ways, worshiped different spirits, and created different art.

As different as the hundreds of Native American groups were from each other, those that lived in similar parts of the Americas shared some of the same traditions. Historians and *archeologists* use the term "**culture area**" (see p. 30) to describe certain geographic regions. People living in these culture areas shared similar ways of life. In North America at least 12 different culture areas existed.

CULTURE AREAS

The Southeast was mild and wet. The warm climate allowed people living there to farm and build large cities.

In the thick forests of the Northeast lived semi-nomads, who built smaller villages when they were not moving from place to place. Although they did some farming, the rocky soil made planting large farms difficult. Therefore, they also hunted, fished, and gathered wild plants and berries.

The Great Plains culture area covers the territory between the Mississippi River and the Rocky Mountains. Although this area contains major rivers, much of the land is flat, grassy *prairie* land. Until the late 1800s, the land was home to millions of buffalo—one of the most important sources of food, clothing, and shelter in Native American life. While some Great Plains nations farmed in small villages along the banks of the Mississippi and other rivers, most were nomads

1800 BCE	**1600 BCE**	**1500 BCE**	**750 BCE**
The first known **Mound Builder** society begins building high mounds or earthworks in Louisiana.	Monumental ceremonial centers begin to be built in South America and Mesoamerica. The societies that build them include the Olmec in Mexico.	During the Postarchaic period, which begins in about 1500 BCE, agriculture spreads, as do villages, pottery, and weaving.	**Mound Builders** known as the Adena and Hopewell peoples build mounds in in the Ohio River valley. In about 100 BCE, they will construct the Serpent Mound near present-day Locust Grove, Ohio.

who followed the buffalo. They hunted buffalo on foot. There were no horses in America until Spanish explorers brought them during the 1500s.

The dry Southwest supported farmers such as the **Hopi** (*HO-pee*) (see p. 34), who lived in pueblos. Because of the dry climate, these Native American farmers grew crops such as corn, beans, and squash. Not all the Native Americans in the Southwest lived in permanent villages. For example, the **Navajo** (*NAH-vuh-ho*) (see p. 41) and **Apache** (*uh-PATCH-ee*) (see p. 22) lived by hunting and by raiding pueblo settlements.

Present-day Idaho, Washington, and Oregon make up the Plateau region. This area features a mix of high mountains, dry prairies, and mighty rivers. Peoples such as the **Nez Percé** (*nez-pur-SAY*) (see p. 41) who lived along the rivers caught fish for their main source of food. Those who lived away from rivers *foraged* for food such as wild onions and potatoes.

Very few plants can grow in the hot and dry Great Basin culture area region of present-day Nevada and Utah. Instead of farming, Native Americans such as the **Paiute** (*PIE-oot*)(see p. 42) and **Shoshone** (*sho-SHO-nee*) (see p. 45) ate by gathering berries, nuts, and roots and by capturing insects and small animals.

The California culture area contains much of modern-day California, along with Baja (*BAH-ha*) California in Mexico. This area was rich with food, including game, fish, shellfish, and wild plants. Native Americans farmed, fished for salmon, and foraged for food such as acorns, which they used in cereal and bread.

100 BCE	300	750	800
The **Anasazi** culture (100 BCE–1300) begins to flourish in the Four Corners region where Colorado, Utah, Arizona, and New Mexico meet. Early on, they show mastery as skilled basket weavers.	In Mesoamerica, the **Maya** begin making advances in astronomy, mathematics, architecture, writing, and agriculture. One pyramid at Tikal rises to 145 feet.	From 750 to their disappearance in 1300, **Anasazi** live in pueblos, multifloored apartment buildings on mesas or in canyons.	**Mound Builders** known as the Mississippians begin to flourish in the Midwest, and last until the early 1600s. They practice intensive agriculture.

To the north of California, the Northwest Coast culture area runs from Alaska south to California. This area was one of the most heavily populated in all the Americas before Europeans came. People living there built canoes to fish and hunt walrus and seals in the ocean. They also caught elk and deer and gathered roots and berries from forests and slopes of mountains.

Two other culture areas are in northern Canada and Alaska. In the Subarctic, in northern Canada, the **Cree** (see p. 29) hunted moose and caribou. In the frozen Arctic, the Aleut (*al-OOT*) and the **Inuit** (*IN-yoo-it*) (see p. 35) fished and hunted seals, whales, and walruses from open boats. They also used trees to build their homes. Further north is an area where no trees grow and the seas are frozen. Here the Inuit hunted seals through holes in the ice and built their homes, known as igloos, out of snow blocks.

The final two regions in North America are the Mesoamerican (*MEZ-oh-American*) culture area and the Circum-Caribbean culture area. The Mesoamerican region stretches from Mexico through Central America and was home to great civilizations such as the Aztec and Maya. The Circum-Caribbean region includes the peoples of the Caribbean, such as the **Arawak** (*AIR-uh-wak*) (see p. 23). The Arawak were the first Native Americans to come in contact with Europeans when Christopher Columbus landed in what are now the Bahama Islands.

From the hot jungles of Central America to the frozen Arctic, this was the world of the Native Americans just before contact with Europe.

1025　1050　1325　ca.1400

1025	1050	1325	ca.1400
Between 1025 and 1400, the ancestors of the **Navajo** and **Apache** begin to migrate southward into the Southwest.	Cahokia, Illinois, is the site of a **Mound Builder** community of up to 50,000 people. They build the largest prehistoric earthwork in North America north of Mexico, Monks Mound, rising to 100 feet.	The **Aztec** found Tenochtitlán (*tay-notch-teet-LAHN*) in what is now Mexico City. Their empire will last until the 16th century.	In the Andes of South America, the **Inca** found an empire that lasts until the 1500s.

A-Z of Key People, Events, and Terms

Abenaki *(ah-buh-NA-kee)*

A group of peoples living in Maine, Vermont, and Quebec. The Abenaki belonged to the Northeast **culture area** (see p. 30). This group included the Maliseet *(MAL-uh-seet)*, Norridgewock *(NOR-idge-wok)*, Passamaquoddy *(pah-suh-muh-KWOD-ee)*, Pennacook *(PENN-uh-cook)*, and Penobscot *(puh-NOB-scot)*. They lived by hunting, fishing, and growing corn. When Europeans arrived, the Abenaki traded with the French allies and helped France fight the British. In 1724–1725, the British destroyed the *confederacy*, with many of the survivors retreating to Quebec.

Alabama and Coushatta *(koo-SHAH-tuh)*

Peoples of the Southeast **culture area** (see p. 30). Sharing a language, they lived in what is now Alabama, the state which bears their name. The Alabama lived on the upper Alabama River in central Alabama. The Coushatta peoples lived in northeastern Alabama. Following wars with Europeans and other Native Americans in the 16th and 17th centuries, both the Alabama and Coushatta fled to eastern Texas, where the Alabama-Coushatta Reservation was established in 1854. They also live today in Oklahoma.

Algonkin *(al-GAHN-kin)*

People of the Northeast **culture area** (see p. 30). They lived mainly by hunting. Their homeland was near the Ottawa River and its northern tributaries in what are now Ontario and Quebec. Before Europeans arrived, the Algonkin were involved in Huron *(HYUR-on)* and Algonquian wars against the Iroquois *(EAR-uh-kwoy)*. Afterward, they were military allies of the French against the British, who were allied with the Iroquois in the **Iroquois Confederacy** (see p. 66).

Anasazi *(ah-nuh-SAH-zee)*

Prehistoric Southwestern people of the Four Corners region. This is the area around where the borders of present-day Colorado, Utah, Arizona, and New Mexico join. The name "Anasazi" means "ancient enemies" or "ancient ones who are not among us." The Anasazi culture began developing about 100 BCE. The early stage of this culture is known as the Basket Maker period because the Anasazi were skillful weavers of baskets, sandals, and other goods. In addition to weaving, they farmed in their villages, and after 400 CE they began making pottery.

From 750 CE to 1300 CE, the Anasazi were in their pueblo period. This is considered their golden age. During this period, they made buildings out of stone and *adobe*. The buildings had many rooms and more than one level. Ladders connected the levels, and the levels were stepped back to form terraces. These *pueblos* (Spanish for towns) were usually built on top of mesas or in canyons. The pueblos in Chaco Canyon, New Mexico, were first inhabited about 900 CE. Chaco's largest building, Pueblo Bonito, had 800 rooms and may have housed more than a thousand people. From 1000 CE to 1300 CE, the Anasazi abandoned free-standing dwellings. They began constructing houses in hollow portions of canyon walls, such as the cliff dwellings at Mesa Verde, Colorado. They probably did this to defend themselves against enemies.

The Anasazi were masters of many crafts, including jewelry, *mosaics*, and cotton-and-feather clothing. They built a network of stone roads like those that connected Chaco Canyon to outlying settlements. They also developed *irrigation* systems to support food production for their large population. In the late 12th century CE, however, they were overwhelmed by drought and attacks from the invading ancestors of the **Apache** (see below) and the **Navajo** (see p. 41). By about 1300, the Anasazi abandoned their cliff dwellings and separated. Some moved south to the Rio Grande Valley, where many of their cultural traits were inherited by the **Pueblo** (see p. 44) peoples.

Remains of cliff dwellings in the Canyon de Chelly, Arizona, home to the Anasazi people in approximately 1200 CE. (National Park Service)

Apache *(uh-PATCH-ee)*

People of the Southwest **culture area** (see p. 30). The Apache arrived in the plains of North America 2,000 years ago. The Apache were hunters and gatherers. They established homelands across the southwestern U.S., mostly in Oklahoma and Arizona. They raided other peoples such as the Pueblo, enslaving them and

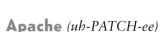

stealing their supplies. Because they were feared as warriors, the Apache slowed the progress of Mexico and of the Spanish who were trying to expand their territory northward. Led by chiefs including **Cochise** (*coh-CHEES*) (see Vol. 2, p. 28) and **Geronimo** (*juh-RON-i-mo*) (see Vol. 2, p. 33), they also battled the large numbers of U.S. troops that entered the Southwest in 1848, after conclusion of the **Mexican-American War** (see Vol. 2, p. 38).

An Apache makes the hand sign for "winter." Sign language was a common form of communication among the nations of the Southwest, who spoke many different languages. (Library of Congress)

Arapaho *(uh-RAP-uh-ho)*

People of the Plains **culture area** (see p. 30). Thousands of years ago, the Arapaho lived in modern-day Canada and Minnesota. They made their living by farming and hunting. Over the next several centuries, they migrated south and west. During this migration the people separated into two groups. These groups settled in parts of modern-day Colorado, Kansas, Nebraska, and Wyoming. Their dealings with the U.S. during the 19th century were marked by violence. Treaties, loss of land, and forced movement to reservations in Oklahoma and Wyoming occurred.

Arawak *(AIR-uh-wak)*

People of the Circum-Caribbean (*SIR-cum-Caribbean*) **culture area** (see p. 30). By the 15th century, the Arawak lived in a wide area, including the West Indies, Florida, and coastal South America. Their enemies, the Carib (*car-EEB*), drove them out of the Lesser Antilles late that century. They were the first Native Americans that Christopher Columbus met when he arrived in the New World in 1492. The Arawak society worshiped spirits who were linked to their social classes, including chiefs and enslaved people. The Arawak lived by farming and fishing. Columbus was welcomed by the Arawak. Later he and the Spanish colonists who followed him attacked and enslaved them. By the end of the 16th century, the Arawak people in the Caribbean islands were killed and their society destroyed. Some Arawak groups survived in South America.

Arikara *(ah-ree-KAR-uh)*

People of the Great Plains **culture area** (see p. 30). The Arikara practiced buffalo hunting, agriculture, and trade. Prior to 1750, they lived in South Dakota. Fleeing Sioux attacks, they migrated north to the border of the Dakotas along the Missouri River. In 1823, the U.S. military drove them into North Dakota, where they were permitted to stay according to the Fort Laramie Treaty of 1851. Arikara still live with the **Mandan** (see p. 37) and **Hidatsa** (see p. 34) in North Dakota, where they are called the Three Affiliated Tribes.

Aztec (*AZ-tek*)

People of the Mesoamerica (*MEZ-oh-America*) **culture area** (see p. 30). According to legend, the Aztec migrated into the Valley of Mexico from Aztlán (*ast-LAHN*). They founded their capital, Tenochtitlán (*tay-notch-teet-LAHN*), now Mexico City, in 1325 CE. The Aztec empire dominated central and southern Mexico from the 14th to the 16th century CE. Their civilization grew because of their military strength, organization, and alliances. The Aztec built pyramids and practiced astronomy and calendar keeping. They encouraged the arts of sculpture, painting, and picture writing. The Aztec worshiped many gods and were known to sacrifice both humans and animals to their gods. Their empire was destroyed by the Spanish in 1521. Aztec descendants still live in Mexico.

Bannock (*BAN-nok*)

People of the Great Basin **culture area** (see p. 30). The Bannock have been linked with the Northern **Shoshone** *(sho-SHO-nee)* (see p. 45) Nation. The two peoples lived as *nomads* and roamed across the mountains and waters of present-day southern Idaho. They made their livings gathering and fishing. Encounters with U.S. settlers in the 19th century were violent. Eventually the Bannock were forced to relocate to an Idaho reservation.

Beaver

People of the Arctic **culture area** (see p. 30). Originally inhabitants of Alberta and British Columbia, they now live in Alaska. Hunters of game, they blended their spiritual beliefs with their searches.

Caddo (*CAD-oh*)

People of the Great Plains **culture area** (see p. 30). Originally part of the Caddo *Confederacy*, or group, the Caddo lived as nomads across present-day Arkansas, Louisiana, Oklahoma, and Texas. Among popular symbols for the Caddo was the turtle. For the Caddo, the turtle symbol represented their legend of the Great Turtle, which saved the Caddo from destruction by monsters. Geometric designs dominate Caddoan craft and clothing. Relations with the U.S. in the 19th century involved resettlement on a reservation in Oklahoma. Since the 20th century, they have sponsored campaigns to retain their tribal status and native lands.

Calusa (*cal-OOS-uh*)

People of the Southeast **culture area** (see p. 30). Inhabitants of modern-day western Florida, the Calusa lived by fishing, hunting, and trading. They were a highly developed culture. The Calusa built canals and they had a finely developed sense of art that can be seen in displays of bead crafts and animal carvings. Throughout their existence, the Calusa strongly defended their land against the Carib (*car-EEB*), who raided them. In the 16th-century invasion by the Spanish, led by explorer Juan Ponce de León, they were finally defeated. Except for a small number who joined other nations, the Calusa culture was destroyed.

Cherokee (*CHAIR-uh-kee*)

People of the Southeast **culture area** (see p. 30). Originally located in what are now the states of Tennessee and North Carolina, the Cherokee lived in log houses and farmed and hunted in the region's rich lands and waterways. Traditional cultural practices included the use of plants for medications and dyes for clothing. Important ceremonies were held in the large building known as the *council house*. Its design and important events held there were influenced by the number seven. It represented the number of groups that originally made up the Cherokee.

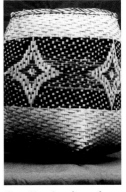

One Cherokee form of craft is basket-weaving. This example was made by a contemporary artist. (Private collection)

As Europeans began to arrive in the 19th century, the Cherokee tried to live among the settlers. In an attempt to demonstrate common ground with the Europeans, the Cherokee created a written version of their language. Although the Cherokee struggled to adapt to European settlers, they were not spared the fate of most Native American nations. In 1838, the settlers' desire for land led to the forced resettling of the Cherokee to Oklahoma. Deadly and long, the trip became known as the **Trail of Tears** (see p. 121).

The Cherokee were one of the **Five Civilized Tribes** (see p. 103), along with the **Chickasaw** (see below), **Choctaw** (see p. 27), **Creek** (see p. 29), and **Seminole** (*SEM-in-ole*) (see p. 116). The Cherokee are now the most populous nation in the U.S., with over 250,000 members.

Cheyenne (*shy-ANN*)

People of the Great Plains **culture area** (see p. 30). Their name is derived from the Lakota (*luh-KO-tuh*) Sioux (*Soo*) term meaning "Different Talkers." The Cheyenne began as hunters in what is modern-day Minnesota but were later driven to the West by the Sioux. The Cheyenne traditionally believe in Maheo (*muh-HEY-oh*) as the creator. His teachings form the basis for their society. With the Sioux, the Cheyenne defeated General George Armstrong Custer's forces at the **Battle of Little Bighorn** (see Vol. 2, p. 37) in 1876. Notable Cheyenne include chief **Black Kettle** (see Vol. 2, p. 22), who worked for peace between his people and the U.S. during the 19th century.

Chickasaw (*CHICK-uh-saw*)

People of the Southeast **culture area** (see p. 30). The Chickasaw Nation dates back nearly 3,000 years. Their origins connect them with the Mississippi **Mound Builders** (see p. 39). Approximately 1,000 years ago, the Chickasaw and **Choctaw** (see p. 27) formed, and much later became members of, the **Five Civilized Tribes** (see p. 103), along with the **Cherokee** (see p. 25), **Creek** (see p. 29), and **Seminole** (see p. 116). The Chickasaw were *nomads* in modern-day Florida and lived as hunters and warriors. Sixteenth-century invasions by Spanish explorers weakened the Chickasaw population. The 19th century brought complete upheaval, as the U.S. government forced them to migrate to Oklahoma.

Chinook (*shi-NOOK*)

People of the Northwest Coast **culture area** (see p. 30). As inhabitants of modern-day Washington and Oregon, the Chinook became known for their trading abilities. They first traded with other native nations, and after the 17th century, they traded with Europeans. In addition to trading, the Chinook

The Flattened Head Tradition

Many nations living in the Columbia River basin of Montana and Idaho, including the people of the Chinook Nation, shared a tradition of flattening the heads of their infants. The procedure was done by placing the child's head between two boards that were tightened with leather ties. The flattened head was thought to be a sign of aristocratic distinction. However, there was one nation living in the region that did not flatten heads. Ironically, the people of this nation were known by their neighbors as the Flathead people, since the tops of their heads were round instead of pointed.

lived by fishing salmon. The salmon later became the symbol of the Chinook. Chinook populations were severely reduced in the 19th century. Many died from illnesses that were introduced by Europeans. In the 20th century, the Chinook began campaigns to reestablish tribal status and other rights related to their livelihood.

Choctaw (*CHOK-taw*)

People of the Southeast **culture area** (see p. 30). One of their myths says that they came from a Mississippi earth mound. Originally inhabitants of Alabama and Mississippi (and later Oklahoma), the Choctaw were farmers. During the War of 1812, they were allies of the U.S. and fought side-by-side with some U.S. troops. They did not join other Southeast Native nations in actions against the U.S., including **Tecumseh's** (*tek-UM-suh*) **Rebellion** (see p. 118) of 1809–1811. Nonetheless, during the early 1830s, they were forced to leave their homeland and sent westward.

Clovis culture

Prehistoric civilization of North America from the *Paleolithic* period. The Clovis culture is named for an *archeological* site near Clovis, New Mexico. The civilization thrived across most of the present-day United States and in parts of Mexico and Canada from

Native American Languages

By the time of Columbus, Native Americans were speaking about 2,200 languages, perhaps 300 of them in the lands north of Mexico. Though many of these languages have died out, some are still spoken, including more than 100 in the United States. Native American languages have given many words to English. Some of the most common are listed below.

English Word	Native American Word	Native American Language Family
Coyote	Coyotl	Nahuatl, a language spoken by many Native Americans of the American Southwest
Canoe	Canoa	Spanish translation from Arawakan, the language of the Arawak
Kayak	Qajaq	Inuit
Llama	Lama peruana	Spanish translation from Quechua, the language of the Inca
Maize	Mahiz	Arawakan
Racoon	arathkone	Algonquian
Squash	Askootasquash	Massachuset, spoken by the Massachuset Nation
Tomato	tomatl	Nahuatl

about 9500 to 8000 BCE. These people hunted mammoths with slender stone spear points that had distinctive *fluting*, or grooves.

Coeur d'Alene (COR-*duh-layn*)

People of the Plateau (*plat-TOH*) **culture area** (see p. 30). The Coeur d'Alene Nation originally inhabited lands along the Columbia and Snake Rivers in Idaho, where they made their living by fishing and hunting and gathering. The Coeur d'Alene began trading with the French and other Europeans. The name Coeur d'Alene refers to a French word for a fellow trader. Relations with the U.S. included a government-supported war between settlers and the Coeur d'Alene during the 1850s. This war resulted in the movement of the Coeur d'Alene to reservations.

Comanche (*cuh-MAN-chee*)

People of the Great Plains **culture area** (see p. 30). The Comanche were originally part of the **Shoshone** (see p. 45) Nation in Wyoming. They migrated south and made their living as hunters of buffalo throughout the Great Plains states, including modern-day Colorado, Kansas, Oklahoma, Texas, and Wyoming. According to legend, the Comanche were created by the *Great Spirit* from the dust of a storm. The Comanche have become known for their abilities and powers as warriors, particularly against Spanish invaders and the U.S. In the 19th century, they waged a 40-year war with the U.S. over sacred lands. The Comanche Nation is now headquartered in Oklahoma.

Cree

People of the Subarctic **culture area** (see p. 30). They inhabit much of what is now Canada and Montana. They lived by hunting and fishing and held strong spiritual beliefs. Interaction with Europeans began in the 17th century when they became advisors to French fur traders in Canada. During the 19th century, the Cree opposed the U.S. and Canada over attempts to regulate hunting.

Creek

People of the Southeast **culture area** (see p. 30). Originally known as the Muskoke (*mus-KO-gee*), the Creek were given their English name by colonists who noted the abundance of creeks in the area. The Creek made their living by farming the rich lands of Alabama and Georgia. Their cultural rituals included the Stomp Dance and Green Corn Ceremony (see sidebar, right). In the 19th century, they were forced to *migrate* to a reservation in Oklahoma.

Green Corn Ceremony

Many northeastern and southeastern nations performed a harvest celebration called the Green Corn Ceremony. For instance, during the celebration, each Creek village would build a small forest of brush and bushes around a rectangular dancing area. They would then light a fire that they considered sacred. Over the next several weeks, a special dance called the Stomp Dance was performed from midnight until dawn of the next day. The people would then cleanse themselves by fasting, scratching themselves with thorns, and drinking the Black Drink, an herb drink containing caffeine.

Crow

People of the Great Plains **culture area** (see below). Originally linked to the Hidatsa, they made their living as farmers in South Dakota. In the 1770s, the Crow formed two groups, the River Crow and Mountain Crow. These groups settled in Montana and Wyoming. In the 18th century, Europeans introduced horses and the development of horse-related crafts emerged as a result. Following the 1851 Fort Laramie Treaty, the Crow gave up their lands and were forced to abandon some traditions. However, since the mid-20th century, the Crow have worked to reestablish their traditions.

culture area

A geographical region with a common environment and similarities in ways of life. Culture areas provide a convenient way to study Native American cultures. The cultures developed differences in their ways of life, but all were closely linked by the land, climate, animals, and plants of their homeland. Native Americans themselves did not think in terms of culture areas, but in terms of their individual nations. These nations sometimes *migrated* from one culture area to another, bringing with them their old ideas and practices as they learned new ones. Still, the concept remains a useful tool for understanding the peoples of the Americas before Columbus. Each culture area shows similarities among the nations that lived there in features such as livelihood, clothing, technology, architecture, arts, religion, politics, games, family life, and war.

There are many ways of dividing North America into culture areas. A common division includes Arctic, California, Circum-Caribbean, Great Basin, Great Plains, Mesoamerica (*MEZ-oh-America*), Northeast, Northwest Coast, Plateau, Southeast, Southwest, and Subarctic (see chart, p. 31 and map, p. 32).

Delaware (*DEL-uh-ware*)

People of the Northeast **culture area** (see above). In recent years, they have become more commonly known by their traditional name, Lenape (*len-AH-pay*), meaning "original people" or "real people." They received the name Delaware from Europeans because they lived along the Delaware River, which was named for British colonial governor Lord De La Warr. The Delaware lived in groups in what are now New Jersey, New York (including

Native American Culture Areas

This chart lists the 12 geographical culture areas that historians and anthropologists (people who study different cultures) often use to study the Native American peoples of North America.

Culture Area	Location	Way of Life
Arctic	Alaska, northern Canada, Greenland	Hunting and fishing; made animal skin tents in summer, igloos in winter during long journeys.
California	California, Baja California	Lived on plants, nuts, small game, shellfish. Families were important social units; formed permanent settlements.
Circum-Caribbean	Caribbean islands, east coast of	Farming and hunting and gathering. Grew cotton Central America for clothing; built thatched roof houses.
Great Basin	Nevada, Colorado, Idaho, Oregon, California, Arizona, New Mexico, Wyoming	Hunted small game and gathered roots, nuts and berries; no agriculture. Small families; some community activities.
Great Plains	Mississippi River valley to Rocky Mountains; parts of Canada south to southern Texas	Originally farmers. After learning horsemanship, became nomadic and buffalo became main source of food and clothing, shelter, and trade.
Meso-america	Mexico and Central America	Highly complex civilizations including Maya, Aztec; large cities.
Northeast	Atlantic seaboard to the Mississippi River valley, Great Lakes to Virginia and North Carolina	Hunter-gatherers, farmers, fishers. Deer main source of food, clothing. Nations usually composed of family clans.
Northwest Coast	Pacific Coast from southeast Alaska to northern California	Fished, hunted, traded. Villages and families formed center of life. Rank determined by material possessions.
Plateau	Parts of of Washington, Oregon, British Columbia, Idaho, Montana, and northern California	Fishing and some hunting; salmon major food source; also wild roots, berries, and vegetation. Independent villages were main social unit.
Southeast	Atlantic Ocean to eastern Texas and Gulf of Mexico northward	Mainly farmers, some hunting and fishing; Some nations descended from ancient Mississippian cultures.
Southwest	Southern Utah and Colorado southward into Mexico	Skilled desert farmers. Some gathered roots, seeds, nuts, berries. Independent villages. Sophisticated art.
Subarctic	Subarctic Canada and Alaska	Nomadic hunters and fishers.

Anthropologists call regions that share similar geography and peoples "culture areas." This map shows one of the most common culture area breakdowns.

Manhattan and Staten Island), Delaware, and eastern Pennsylvania. They lived by farming, hunting, and fishing. The Delaware enjoyed a special status among people who spoke Algonquian (*al-GAHN-kwee-in*) languages. They were regarded as grandfathers of the other Algonquian nations and peacemakers between the nations of the **Iroquois** (*EAR-uh-kwoy*) **Confederacy** (see p. 66) and the Algonquians. Perhaps because of this, they differed from other Algonquians in not preparing their villages for defense. At first they largely enjoyed peaceful relations with European colonists, particularly in Pennsylvania, where they signed a treaty of friendship with governor **William Penn** (see p. 77) in 1682. But they were gradually pushed west to Ohio, Oklahoma, and Ontario.

Flathead

People of the Plateau **culture area** (see p. 30). Originally hunters and gatherers in modern-day Montana, the Flathead were also highly spiritual and skilled at crafts. Beginning in the 18th century, they met Europeans, who introduced horses to Flathead culture. They may have earned the name Flathead from their practice of allowing their children's heads to shape naturally, in contrast to neighboring nations that shaped their children's heads into points through the use of braces (see sidebar, page 27).

Gros Ventre (*grow-vant*)

People of the Plains **culture area** (see p. 30). Originally inhabitants of modern-day Wyoming, the Gros Ventre were traders and farmers. They eventually moved northward to Montana. It was trading with the French that gave the Gros Ventre their name. It comes from a French translation of the name of the river (Big Belly) that flowed near their trading site. The Gros Ventre believe in *World maker* as their creator and offer him gifts and ceremonies throughout the year. The group was also respected as warriors. In the 19th century, they suffered from diseases that were spread by the Europeans.

Haida (*HI-duh*)

People of the Northwest Coast **culture area** (see p. 30). The Haida were established in Alaska and British Columbia, and they now reside in Alaska and Washington. Originally, they lived by fishing and trading. They were known for their intricate carving of cedar. In the 19th century, European settlers brought lumber mills, canneries, and trading posts to their homeland. Like many Northwest Coast peoples, they are known for carved *totem poles*. (See sidebar, right.)

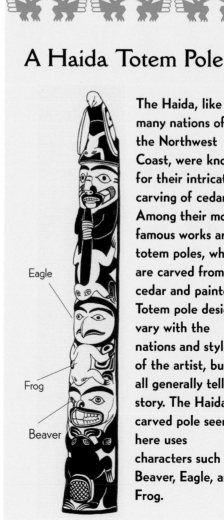

A Haida Totem Pole

The Haida, like many nations of the Northwest Coast, were known for their intricate carving of cedar. Among their most famous works are totem poles, which are carved from cedar and painted. Totem pole designs vary with the nations and style of the artist, but all generally tell a story. The Haida carved pole seen here uses characters such as Beaver, Eagle, and Frog.

Eagle

Frog

Beaver

Hidatsa (*he-DOT-suh*)

People of the Great Plains **culture area** (see p. 30). The Hidatsa originally lived along the Missouri River. They moved northward into North Dakota, where they made their living through the 18th century by hunting and farming beans, corn, and tobacco. Their cultural practices included communicating with the crops and catching eagles. In the 19th century, the Hidatsa moved farther north but were struck hard by an 1837 cholera *epidemic*. Dealings with the U.S. were marked by the 1851 Fort Laramie Treaty, which forced them to move to a reservation in North Dakota.

Hopi (*HO-pee*)

People of the Southwest **culture area** (see p. 30). The Hopi are descendants of the **Anasazi** (see p. 21). They have lived and farmed in *adobe* communities in modern-day Arizona and New Mexico since before Columbus arrived in 1492. Spiritual practices center on respect for their creator, Masau-u (*mas-OW-oo*). The Hopi beliefs include promises they have made to Masau-u to preserve their environment and avoid a Great Purification that will destroy the earth. Many Hopi cultural practices center on the *kachina* (*kuh-CHEE-nuh*), or ancestor spirit. Such practices include seasonal celebrations and the use of kachina figures.

A Hopi kachina doll symbolizes the spirit of the ancestors. (Private collection)

Huron (*HYUR-on*)

A confederacy, or group, of nations in the Northeast **culture area** (see p. 30). Their group arose in Ontario, Canada, possibly beginning in the 15th century. In rich lands along the Atlantic, they lived in *longhouses*. The Huron lived by farming, hunting, and trading. Traditionally, the Iroquois (see **Iroquois Confederacy**, p. 66) were their enemies. In the 17th century, the Huron became allies of the French. Common Huron cultural practices include needlework, which they learned from the Europeans, and ritual pipe smoking.

Inca (*IN-cuh*)

People of South America's Central and Southern Andes **culture area** (see p. 30). In about 1100 CE, they began to move from the south highland region into the Valley of Cuzco (*KOOS-ko*), Peru. Their ruler was called the Inca, or "king," a name that came to include the entire people. Gradually, they dominated the people around them. The Inca empire expanded quickly, stretching through the Andes Mountains from Ecuador to Argentina. In the early 1500s, the empire grew to its largest under Huayna Capac (*WY-nuh cuh-PAK*). At its height, the empire measured more than 2,500 miles from north to south and 500 miles from east to west. The society was structured by class and practiced animal and human sacrifice. The Inca emperors were viewed as representatives of the sun god and had absolute power. Inca accomplishments included a network of stone roads, *irrigation* canals, temples and palaces, and rope suspension bridges. They were skilled in art, music, metalwork, and agriculture. After Huayna's death, the empire fell into civil war. The Spanish killed the last Inca emperor, Atahualpa, in 1533.

The Incas' last emperor, Atahualpa, was killed by Spanish invaders. (Library of Congress)

Inuit (*IN-yoo-it*)

People of the Arctic **culture area** (see p. 30). The Inuit homeland spans from Greenland to part of Alaska and includes three oceans—the Arctic, Atlantic, and Pacific. The Inuit may have entered the area from the Bering Strait some time between 3000 and 1000 BCE. The Inuit are divided into two groups, the Yupik (*YOO-pik*) and the Inupiat (*in-OO-pee-at*). The Yupik traditionally lived in the less harsh Pacific Coast region of Alaska and made their living hunting, fishing, and whaling. If wood was available, many lived in above-ground dwellings. In contrast, the Inupiat lived along the Arctic edges of Alaska, Canada, and Greenland. Because the Inupiat land lacked trees, the people sometimes built ice houses, known as *igloos*. The Inuit traditionally use dogs to pulls sleds and to sniff through ice for seals. They have strong beliefs in higher powers that help them to endure their rough physical life. A common name for Inuit is Eskimo (*ES-ki-mo*), though many prefer Inuit.

Ioway (*AY-o-way*)

People of the Plains **culture area** (see p. 30). Traders, hunters of buffalo, and planters of corn, the Ioway lived in Iowa, Minnesota, and Missouri until the mid-19th century. They were

The Origin of the Kiowa

According to the Kiowa, a Plains nation, their history began when Saynday (*SAY-un-day*), a mythical folk hero, found them in a hollow cottonwood tree and led them out. In Kiowa legend, Saynday is both superhuman and humorous. Thus, he represents different aspects of the people's personality. Saynday later provided his people with Pahy (*PAH-hee*), the Sun.

Saynday was coming along in darkness upon the face of the sunless earth. He was both lonely and curious as he wandered in a world without people and animals.

Stumbling along, he stretched out his arms and felt something. Carefully probing with his hands and fingers, he recognized the rough surface of a cottonwood tree. Tired and discouraged, Saynday stopped to rest.

As Saynday relaxed, he heard strange sounds coming from beneath the hollow cottonwood tree. Rapping on it, he called out, "Who is there? Who are you?"

"We are people. We want to come out into your world. Help us," came the answer.

Surprised and excited, Saynday reached through an opening of the hollow tree into the underground darkness. Holding out his hand, he clasped the hand of the person nearest him and instructed everyone else to do the same, thus forming a chain of people.

Saynday pulled the first person through a hole in the trunk made by a Sawpole (Owl), and he watched in amazement as the people poured out like ants. After some had emerged, a pregnant female became stuck in the opening of the hole and could go neither forward nor backward. She blocked the way for those behind her and no more came out....

Those who came from that hollow cottonwood tree became the Principal People of the Kiowas. And because the pregnant female prevented all of the people from coming out into the world, the Kiowas have always been a small tribe.

Source: Frederick J. Reuss, *Saynday Was Coming Along.*

forced to resettle in Kansas, Nebraska, and Oklahoma. They traded with the French during the 18th century.

Iroquois *(EER-uh-kwoy)* **Confederacy**
(See p. 66)

Kiowa *(KI-uh-wuh)*
People of Plains **culture area** (see p. 30). The Kiowa lived near the Red, Canadian, and Arkansas rivers in what are now Texas, Oklahoma, Kansas, New Mexico, and Colorado. As *nomads*, they

hunted and moved to the Great Plains during the 18th century. They probably came from the mountains of the upper Missouri River in Montana. They became allies of the **Comanche** (see p. 29) and also of the nation of **Apaches** (see p. 22) called Kiowa Apache. The Kiowa were known for their skill in warfare and for their *pictographic* system of signs. They used these signs as calendars to note important events. In the later 19th century, they were involved in the **Kiowa Wars** (see Vol. 2, p. 29) with the U.S. They were defeated in 1875 and now live principally in Oklahoma.

Klamath (*KLAM-uth*)

People of the Plateau **culture area** (see p. 30). Known as the People of the Lake, the Klamath lived along the Klamath River in modern-day California and Oregon. They made their living fishing and gathering. The Klamath adopted practices from peoples of nearby regions, such as verbal skills from the **Modoc** (see p. 39) of the California culture area. In 1869, they were forced onto a reservation. In the mid-20th century, the U.S. ended Klamath tribal status, but reinstated the status in the 1980s.

Kutchin (*KOO-chin*)

People of the Subarctic **culture area** (see p. 30). Known as the People of the Deer, the Kutchin live in Alaska. They traditionally lived by hunting and fishing. In recent times, they have lived with other people in the same region, including the **Beaver** (see p. 24).

Mandan (*MAN-dun*)

People of the Plains **culture area** (see p. 30). The Mandan were originally inhabitants of modern-day North Dakota. They made their living by vegetable farming and hunting for buffalo. In the 19th century, they suffered from loss of land and diseases spread by Europeans. The Mandan Nation began to disappear after the damming of the Missouri River in the mid-20th century. Those who remain together in North Dakota still engage in traditional cultural practices such as dances and decorative craft work.

A cast of a Mayan head sculpture, found at the ancient site of Palenque on the Yucatán Peninsula of Mexico. (Museum of Natural History)

Maya (*MY-uh*)

Group of peoples belonging to the Mesoamerica (*MEZ-oh-America*) **culture area** (see p. 30). Based in Mexico's Yucatán

(Yoo-kuh-TAHN) Peninsula, the Maya formed a civilization in about 1500 BCE that reached to Guatemala, Honduras, and Belize. Between about 300 CE and 900 CE, they built pyramids and made advances in agriculture, astronomy, mathematics, pottery, copper and gold ornaments, and architecture. Their city-state capitals, including Tikal *(tee-KAHL)*, Copán *(co-PAHN)*, and Palenque *(pal-EN-kay)*, had ceremonial centers that were dedicated to their gods. After 900 CE, many southern Mayan cities were mysteriously abandoned, but Maya continued to live in the Yucatán. During this time, cities such as Chama *(CHAH-muh)* and Chichén Itzá, *(chee-CHIN eet-SUH)* reached their height of prosperity. In the 1500s, the Spanish conquered the largest Mayan groups, though some smaller ones remained independent until the early 20th century.

Menominee *(muh-NOM-uh-nee)*

People of the Northeast **culture area** (see p. 30). The Menominee were originally divided into *clans*, particularly the Bears and Thunderers. They lived in modern-day Michigan and Wisconsin. These clans hunted and gathered, planted, and held spirit celebrations. Beginning in the 18th century, European diseases reduced their numbers. In the mid-20th century, the U.S. temporarily removed their *tribal status* (see **termination policy**, Vol 2, p. 119). The Menominee now live in Wisconsin.

Miami

People of the Southeast **culture area** (see p. 30). The Miami were an alliance of five bands of peoples who were hunters and farmers. They originally made their living along the waters of Indiana. Cultural practices included training children for adulthood and honoring sacred animals. Conflicts with settlers arose over European expansion over the Ohio River. This resulted in a battle at Fallen Timbers in 1794, in which the Miami and other Great Lakes groups were defeated. In the mid-19th century, the Miami split into two groups, the Eastern Miami and Western Miami. They reside today in Indiana and Oklahoma, respectively.

Miwok *(MEE-wok)*

People of the California **culture area** (see p. 30). The Miwok lived in central California, where they were traders and hunter-gatherers. Like other peoples of the area, they participated in seasonal celebrations such as Big Time, which is still practiced today (see sidebar, at right). Interaction with Europeans began in the 16th century, with the Spanish, who placed some Miwok in missions (see **missionaries** p. 70). In the following century, Russian fur traders arrived, and in the 19th century, so did U.S. gold prospectors. All the European groups attempted to control the region, and all brought fatal diseases such as *smallpox* to the Miwok. The battles against white settlers included the 1850–1851 Mariposa Indian War. Miwok uprisings against settlers and fatal diseases introduced by the Europeans reduced the Miwok numbers by over two-thirds by the middle of the 1800s.

Modoc *(MO-dock)*

People of the Plateau **culture area** (see p. 30). The Modoc were formerly inhabitants of what are now Canada and Oregon. They lived by hunting and fishing. In the 1860s and 1870s, they were moved to reservations in Oregon and Oklahoma. From 1954 until the late 1970s, the Modoc lost their tribal standing.

Mojave *(Mo-HAV-ee)*

People of the Southwest **culture area** (see p. 30). The Mojave have lived in Arizona, Nevada, and California, making their livelihoods hunting, fishing, and farming along the Colorado River. By the early 20th century, *diseases* introduced by the Europeans had nearly wiped out the Mojave, reducing their numbers by 90 percent.

Mound Builders

Ancient peoples of the *Postarchaic (post-arh-KAY-ic)* period, the Mound Builders were named for the large mounds they built for burial or ceremonial purposes. They lived in areas from the

Big Time

Each summer for hundreds of years, Native Americans from the Miwok, Maidu, and Pomo nations have celebrated what they call the Big Time ceremony. Traditionally, Big Time was a monthlong chance to see old friends, make new ones, and celebrate together with feasts, dancing, and trading. People from nations throughout what is now the San Francisco Bay area would meet at an agreed site. They brought with them portable shelter, food to share at the feast, tools for hunting and making food, and items to trade such as baskets and precious stones. The Big Time celebration still takes place every year.

Cultures in the Mississippi and Ohio River valleys used man-made mounds of earth as temples or tombs. Most are small, but the snakelike Great Serpent Mound in Ohio stretches for almost a quarter of a mile. (National Park Service)

Great Lakes to the Gulf of Mexico. The Mound Builders farmed, made beautiful artifacts, and had complex societies. The earliest known culture of Mound Builders was the Poverty Point culture in Louisiana, which lasted from 1800 BCE until about 500 BCE. Later Mound Builders included the Adena *(uh-DEE-nuh)* in the Ohio River valley (1000 BCE–200 CE) and the Hopewell in the Ohio and Illinois River valleys (200 BCE–700 CE). Another group, the Mississippian culture, lived in an area that stretched from the Southeast as far north as Wisconsin from 800 CE until the 1600s. In addition to building mounds, they built large towns, such as Cahokia *(cuh-HO-kee-uh)*, Illinois, where up to 50,000 people lived (1050 CE–1250). Mounds came in many shapes, including pyramids, cones, and animals. An example is the Great Serpent Mound, built by the Adena culture near Peebles, Ohio.

Natchez *(NATCH-ez)*
People of the Southeast culture area (see p. 30). The Natchez have a long history, as they are descendants of the Mound Builders (see p. 39). They were sun worshipers who believed

their chief was a direct descendant of the sun god. They lived by trading and farming. They began trading with the French in the 17th century. Warfare with the French reduced their numbers. The last native speaker died in 1965.

Navajo (*NAH-vuh-ho*)

A young Navajo, photographed about 1900. (National Archives)

People of the Southwest **culture area** (see p. 30). Navajo ancestors were originally inhabitants of the Subarctic region. They moved into the Southwest after 1000 CE. By the 17th century, the Navajo were making their living herding and hunting in Southwest. They now live on a three-state-wide reservation in Arizona, New Mexico, and Utah. The Navajo are skilled crafters and work as silversmiths and weavers. Navajo sand paintings illustrate their spiritual beliefs. Many Navaho prefer the name Dineh *(dee-NUH)*, which means "the people," when referring to themselves.

Nez Percé (*nez-pur-SAY*)

People of the Plateau **culture area** (see p. 30). Originally living in Idaho, Montana, and Washington, the Nez Percé were hunters-gatherers and fishers. They were the most powerful people of the Plateau area. In the 19th century, they fought fiercely to save their land. Protecting and preserving the earth is displayed in many of their legends. The Nez Percé name derives from the French term "pierced nose," even though the people did not pierce their noses.

Ojibwa (*oh-JIB-way*)

People of the Northeast **culture area** (see p. 30). One of the largest Native American nations north of Mexico, their homeland stretched from Michigan to Montana and into southern Canada. According to the Ojibwa, they moved from the St. Lawrence River valley and were related to the Ottawa *(OT-uh-wuh)* and Potawatomi *(pot-uh-wah-TOW-mee)*. They were organized in clans, with one clan claiming to be the chiefs of the entire nation. They lived in ***wigwams*** and supported themselves by hunting and gathering, fishing, and farming. In the **French and Indian War** (see p. 61), they sided with the French. They sided with the British in the **American Revolution** (see p. 99) and **War of 1812** (see p. 123).

Powwows

Although the word "powwow" is sometimes used by non–Native Americans to mean an important meeting, to Native Americans, powwow means something more. To them, powwows are gatherings of Native Americans to visit, sing, feast, and dance together.

Traditional Pueblo dancers at a modern-day powwow in New Mexico. (New Mexico Department of Tourism/Dan Monaghan)

The first powwows, which many believe were begun by the Omaha of the Great Plains, were probably held in the late 1800s. Early powwows were probably war dances. Once most Native American nations moved onto reservations, powwows became social events.

Clothing worn by powwow dancers has also changed. Originally, the special headdresses, feathers, and other clothing worn at powwows were worn only by proven warriors. Today, at modern powwows, all men and boys can wear these costumes as a way of honoring their Native American heritage. In the same way, clothing worn by women and girls at today's powwows is a modern version of traditional clothing, usually made of buckskin leather or cloth.

Although most modern powwows are open to the general public, Native Americans do not think of them as entertainment. Instead, they are seen as a way for Native Americans to share and support their traditions.

Omaha (*OH-muh-ha*)

People of the Great Plains **culture area** (see p. 30). The Omaha have lived for centuries in what is now Nebraska and have made their living as farmers and hunters. Into the 19th century, they lived in *earth lodge*s. Among their cultural practices is the celebration known as the powwow, which the Omaha are believed to have originated. Encounters with the U.S. included the exploration of **Lewis and Clark** (see p. 110) in 1803 and ongoing campaigns to maintain U.S. government-Omaha treaties.

Paiute (*PIE-oot*)

People of the Great Basin **culture area** (see p. 30). The Paiute lived as nomads, hunting and gathering across the north and west. Composed of two groups, the Northern Paiute and the Southern

Paiute, their lands spanned Arizona, California, Nevada, Oregon, and Utah. Their homes consisted of temporary *wickiups (WICK-ee-ups)*. In the 19th century, the United States took much of the Paiute land. In 1954, the Paiute lost their *tribal status*.

Pawnee (*PAW-nee* or *paw-NEE*)

People of the Great Plains **culture area** (see p. 30). Residents of what is now Nebraska and Wyoming, the Pawnee built *earth lodges* and lived by farming and hunting. Their traditional enemies were the **Sioux** (see p. 46), against whom they fought with the U.S. Relations with the U.S. were usually good, but settlers brought *disease* that cut the Pawnees' numbers. They were removed to Oklahoma in the mid-1870s.

Pequot (*PEE-kwat*)

People of the Northeast **culture area** (see p. 30). Located in modern-day Connecticut, the Pequot lived by farming, hunting, and gathering. They often fought other local nations, over territory and trade. Interaction with Europeans began in the 17th century, as traders and settlers entered the region. In the 1630s, the deaths of two traders led to the **Pequot War** (see p. 78), which came to an end with attack on a Pequot village in May 1637. It resulted in over 600 deaths and the selling of many Pequot into slvery in Bermuda.

Pomo (*PO-mo*)

People of the California **culture area** (see p. 30). Situated in present-day California, the Pomo made their living by hunting, gathering, and fishing along the northern area's rich lands. Among their crafts was basket weaving. Both children and adults worked to create simple baskets as well as complex designs that interwove shells, beads, and feathers. Interaction with Europeans began during the 19th century. Russian settlers attempted to control the Pomo, use their labor, and command the fur trade in the region. In 1812, the Russians set up Fort Ross for their fur trade. Their harsh treatment of the Pomo increased, and the Pomo began to fight back with various types of violent resistance. In 1841, the Pomo won a short-term victory when the Russians left the camp.

Powhatan Confederacy

Confederacy of tribes in the Southeast **culture area** (see p. 30). The Powhatan originally lived in Virginia and throughout the middle Atlantic region. They made their living hunting, gathering, and farming. In the 17th century, the Powhatan shared farming skills with English colonists. They introduced the settlers to useful crops such as corn and tobacco. Later, English settlers and the Powhatan went to war. Notable members of the Powhatan are Chief Powhatan and Pocahontas (*poke-uh-HAHN-tus*), one of his daughters. The Powhatan, reduced in number by *diseases* introduced by the Europeans, now live in New Jersey.

Pueblo (*PWEB-lo*)

Group of peoples of the Southwest **culture area** (see p. 30). Several nations linked by history but differing in cultural practices make up the Pueblo, such as the Acoma (*AH-cuh-muh*); **Hopi** (*HO-pee*) (see p. 34); Taos (*touse*); and Zuñi (*ZOO-nee*). Originally, the Pueblo were located across Arizona, Colorado, New Mexico, Utah, Texas, and Mexico. They lived by farming and hunting. Many lived in houses made of *adobe* (clay mud) bricks, which had many rooms and levels.

English colonist John Smith captures Chief Powhatan. (Library of Congress)

Historically, many Pueblo groups descend from the Cliff Dwellers, or **Anasazi** (see p. 21). Up until the 14th century, when they left the area, the Anasazi lived in large numbers across the Southwest and worked as large-scale farmers and artisans. Later Pueblo peoples followed Anasazi farming and craft practices such as pottery.

Interaction with Europeans began in the 16th century when the Spanish arrived in New Mexico to take control. In the 17th century, the aim of the Spanish was to conquer the Pueblo and convert them to Christianity. The move to convert them and curb their traditional religious practices led to the **Pueblo Revolt** (see p. 84) in 1680, which temporarily drove the Spanish from the area.

The word *pueblo* means town or village in Spanish. Currently, Pueblo numbers stand at about 40,000.

Seminole (*SEM-in-ole*)

See p. 116.

Many Pueblo peoples lived in multiroom, multistory adobe (clay mud) houses. (National Archives)

Shawnee (*shaw-NEE*)

People of the Northeast **culture area** (see p. 30). The Shawnee originated in the mid-South near the Savannah River. They moved northward in the 17th century and later west into the Ohio River valley. They lived by farming and hunting and gathering. Allies of the British during the **American Revolution** (see p. 99), they continued to battle the U.S. during the **War of 1812** (see p. 123) and spent much of the rest of the 19th century fighting against U.S. expansion west of the Ohio River.

Shoshone (*sho-SHO-nee*)

People of the Southwest **culture area** (see p. 30). The Shoshone originally made their living as hunters and gatherers in several southwestern states. They became known as healers. Their ceremonies included the Sun Dance, War Dance, and Grass Dance, some of which were adapted from other Native American regions. Notable Shoshone members include Sacajawea *(sack-uh-juh-WAY-uh)*, who acted as a translator for U.S. explorers Meriwether Lewis and William Clark in the early 19th century.

The Lakota Love of Nature

Native Americans have a special relationship with nature. Traditionally, they view all natural things—plants, animals, and the inanimate world—as having spirits or souls of their own, like human beings. Humans have a kinship to nature, depend on it for their sustenance, and owe it reverence. Here, Luther Standing Bear (1868–1939), a Lakota Sioux, tells about his people's relationship to the earth.

The Lakota was a true naturalist — a lover of Nature. He loved the earth and all things of the earth, and the attachment grew with age. The old people came literally to love the soil and they sat or reclined on the ground with a feeling of being close to a mothering power. It was good for the skin to touch the earth, and the old people liked to remove their moccasins and walk with bare feet on the sacred earth.

Their tipis were built upon the earth and their altars were made of earth. The birds that flew in the air came to rest upon the earth, and it was the final abiding place of all things that lived and grew. The soil was soothing, strengthening, cleansing, and healing.

This is why the old Indian still sits upon the earth instead of propping himself up and away from its life-giving forces. For him, to sit or lie upon the ground is to be able to think more deeply and to feel more keenly; he can see more clearly into the mysteries of life and come closer in kinship to other lives about him.

Source: Luther Standing Bear, *The Living Spirit of the Indian.*

Sioux *(soo)*

Confederacy of the Plains **culture area** (see p. 30). The Sioux identify themselves by their major subdivisions, the Dakota, Lakota *(luh-KO-tuh)*, and Nakota *(nuh-KO-tuh)*. From 1300 to the 18th century, the Sioux lived in the woodlands along the Mississippi River in Minnesota, where they hunted small game, fished, and farmed. Conflict with the **Ojibwa** (see p. 41) forced them to move to the northern Great Plains, in an area that included what are now North and South Dakota, Montana, and part of Canada. There they became expert bison hunters. They were allies of the British during the **American Revolution** (see p. 99) and **War of 1812** (see p. 123). They later clashed repeatedly with U.S. forces, notably at **Little Bighorn** (1876) (see Vol. 2, p. 37) and **Wounded Knee** (1890) (see Vol. 2, p. 54).

Timucua (*tim-uh-KOO-uh*)

People of the Southeast **culture area** (see p. 30). One of the earliest known Native groups, the Timucua were settled along the west coast of modern-day Florida as early as the first century BCE. They lived by fishing and gathering. Their villages protected them from attacks from other native groups. The Timucua incurred great losses during the 16th century in battles with Spanish conquerors such as Juan Ponce de León. Illness and *diseases* introduced by the Europeans also cut their numbers. By the beginning of the 18th century, they were completely eliminated.

Tlingit (*TLING-git*)

People of the Northwest Coast **culture area** (see p. 30). The Tlingit originally lived across Canada's Yukon Territory and in British Columbia and Alaska. They were reduced in number by smallpox *epidemics* during the 19th century. Today they live mainly in Washington and Oregon.

Umatilla (*oom-uh-TILL-uh*)

People of the Plateau **culture area** (see p. 30). The Umatilla originally made their living through hunting and fishing, particularly for salmon. The Umatilla held yearly celebrations of their creator and his gifts (in the forms of vegetation and salmon). In the 18th century, Europeans introduced horses to the Umatilla.

Ute (*YOOT*)

People of the Great Basin **culture area** (see p. 30). The Ute were located in modern-day Colorado and Utah. They lived by hunting and gathering. The Ute conducted regular raids on nearby groups including Spanish, the **Arapaho** (see p. 23), and, centuries earlier, the **Anasazi** (see p. 21). Interaction with Europeans began in the 1600s, as the Spanish entered Ute territory. In the mid- to late-1800s, the U.S. government placed the Ute on reservations in Colorado and Utah. U.S. silver miners hoping to control Ute lands also created pressure to relocate the Ute. Notable conflicts with the U.S. include the Ute War (1879).

Wampanoag *(wam-puh-NO-ag)*

New England nation of the Northeast **culture area** (see p. 30). Situated in Rhode Island along Narragansett Bay, the Wampanoag lived in *wigwams* and were expert farmers and fishers. They shared their knowledge with the Pilgrims from England and helped them survive their first season in the Plymouth Colony. The Wampanoag celebrated the first Thanksgiving with these settlers. Later, they fought them during **King Philip's War** (see p. 69) in 1675–1676.

Winnebago *(win-uh-BAY-go)*

People of the Northeast **culture area** (see p. 30). According to legend, the first Winnebago were created by spirit and human forces in Wisconsin. They were organized into two *clans* and lived by farming, hunting, and gathering in Wisconsin and Nebraska. When they began trading with Europeans in the 17th century, Winnebago ranks were greatly diminished by European-introduced diseases.

Yakima *(YAH-kee-muh)*

People of the Plateau **culture area** (see p. 30). Living by fishing, the Yakima originally were in a mountainous region of modern-day Washington. According to native legends, the Yakima were assigned this rough terrain by an angry creator. The Yakima have had strong beliefs in spirits who were associated with the surrounding mountains. They continue to follow traditional cultural practices, such as the use of cradleboards to carry infants and deerskin or canvas wing dresses for women. Confrontations with U.S. settlers and military during the mid-19th century reduced Yakima numbers.

Yokuts *(YO-cuts)*

People of the California **culture area** (see p. 30). Situated in the present-day San Joaquin *(wah-KEEN)* Valley in California, they lived by hunting and gathering. Cultural practices included seasonal dances and celebrations and intricate rituals to mark deaths and other life experiences. Into the 17th century, there were up to 60 *bands* in the area. Interaction with settlers brought conflict and diseases. These two conditions reduced the Yokuts' numbers by three-fourths. Conflict with the U.S. included the 1850–1851 Mariposa Indian War.

CHAPTER TWO

A Clash of Worlds

Colonization and Conquest, 1492–1763

"When you first came to our coasts, you sometimes had no food; we gave you our beans and corn, and relieved you with our oysters and fish; and now, for recompense, you murder our people."

—Anonymous Montauk, 17th century

The arrival of **Christopher Columbus** (see p. 60) in the Bahamas in 1492 was the beginning of a long period of change for Native Americans. Gradually, they came to know the European strangers. Most Native Americans reacted to Europeans with help and advice about the land. Sometimes the newcomers were kind to them in return, sometimes not. European settlers eventually brought lasting change and destruction to the Native Americans' ways of life. The meeting of new and old worlds always became a clash of worlds.

Although Columbus was Italian-born, he sailed as a Spanish explorer. Columbus opened the way for other Europeans to explore and colonize the New World. He also set a pattern that was repeated over and over. Contact with Europeans ended with European conquest of the Native American nations. This pattern was always the same, but the details and pace of the conquests varied greatly from place to place.

In the case of Columbus, who made four voyages to the New World, conquest was swift. The **Arawak** (*AIR-uh-wak*) (see p. 23) people he first met in the West Indies wore gold ornaments in their noses. This was a sign that gold lay nearby. Columbus began to colonize the large island of Hispaniola (*his-pan-ee-OH-la*) with the aim of searching for gold. The

Spanish treated the native people cruelly, and within a few years Hispaniola was conquered.

THE SPANISH IN THE NEW WORLD

Spanish firearms, steel swords, horses, and war dogs were important in their New World conquests. However, European diseases proved to be even more deadly. Contact with Europeans introduced Native Americans to ailments such as smallpox, measles, and typhus. Native Americans had no natural immunity to, or ability to resist, these diseases. More Native Americans died from the diseases than were lost in wars.

In due course, the Spanish conquered the other large islands of the Caribbean, including Puerto Rico, Jamaica, and Cuba. Everywhere they went, they killed, robbed, and enslaved the local Native Americans. In 1542, just 50 years after Columbus first arrived, Spanish priest Bartolomé de Las Casas (*bar-TAHL-oh-may day lahs CAHS-uhs*) wrote: "All those islands…are now abandoned and desolate."

By then, Spanish *conquistadors* (cone-*KEES-tuh-doors*) had reached the mainland. Native Americans resisted, and won some victories. The Maya (see p. 37) of the Yucatán (*yoo-cuh-TAHN*) Peninsula defeated and killed Spaniard Francisco Fernández de Córdoba (*COR-doh-buh*). But everywhere in the New World, more Europeans came to replace those killed. Hernán Cortés (*cor-TEZ*) conquered the Aztec (see p. 24) Empire of Mexico.

Timeline

1492

Italian-born Spanish explorer **Christopher Columbus** reaches the West Indies. During his four voyages (1492–1504), he founds a colony in Hispaniola, where the Spanish attack and enslave Native Americans.

1508–1511

The Spanish conquer Puerto Rico, Jamaica, and Cuba. Within decades, Native Americans in the West Indies are all but wiped out.

Francisco Pizarro began the conquest of the Inca (see p. 34) Empire of Peru. The Spanish ventured deep into South America, Central America, and North America. In North America, they founded the colonies of St. Augustine, Florida, and San Juan de los Caballeros (*cahb-ay-AIR-os*), New Mexico.

In most of these places, local Native Americans were forced to work. One such work arrangement was called the ***encomienda*** (*ehn-coh-mee-EHN-da*) system. Under this plan, a group of Native Americans would be assigned to work for a Spanish settler. Native Americans were also forced to practice Christianity. Many Native American women were forced to become the mistresses or wives of their conquerors. They gave birth to a new mixed race. This mixed race today makes up a large part of the population of Latin America.

Spain became rich with gold and silver mined by Native Americans. Other European nations saw opportunities for profit. Portugal claimed Brazil and began to colonize. Their colonization resulted in the destruction of the local Tupinambá (*too-pi-nahm-BUH*) people. Jacques Cartier of France explored the Gulf of St. Lawrence in Canada. He traded with Micmac and Huron (see p. 34). He was followed by Samuel de Champlain, who founded Quebec City in Canada in 1608. British explorer Francis Drake explored near present-day San Francisco. He found the local Native Americans "people of a tractable, free and loving nature, without guile or treachery"—and he claimed their land for Great Britain.

1521	1531–1535	1534	1542
Spanish conquistador Hernán Cortés conquers the Aztec Empire in Mexico.	Spanish conquistador Francisco Pizarro conquers the Inca Empire in Peru.	French explorer Jacques Cartier trades with Micmac and Huron in Canada.	Under pressure from priest Bartolomé de Las Casas, Spain enacts the New Laws, prohibiting enslavement of Native Americans and providing for better treatment. The laws are never fully enforced.

Wherever they went, Europeans claimed the land, but settling the land was not as easy. In the 16th century, both France and England tried and failed to establish settlements in what is now the United States. France failed with Fort Caroline, Florida. England failed in two attempts with Roanoke Island, North Carolina, in 1585 and 1587.

In the 17th century, the pace of European colonization in North America increased. Beginning with Jamestown, Virginia, England founded colonies along the Atlantic coast. Each colony was loyal to the king but free to set up its own form of local government. Immigrants were welcome and opportunities for advancement great. The British colonies grew quickly, reaching a population of 85,000 by 1672.

France's North American empire, **New France** (see map, p. 56), had reached a population of only 6,700 by the same date. The difference was that New France discouraged immigration, and laws were enforced by tight central control. France had reason to avoid too much settlement. New France's main economic activity was trading with Native Americans. In return for goods like steel knives, steel kettles, woolen blankets, and guns, the Huron and **Algonkin** (*al-GAHN-kin*) (see p. 21) offered beaver fur. The fur was used in making hats that were popular in Europe. New France needed to leave the forest homeland of the beaver and its Huron and Algonquian trappers untouched.

New France's relations with its Native American trading and military allies were friendly. This was not the case in the British colonies. The British

1570	**1579**	**1607**	**1617–1619**
In New York, five nations form the **Iroquois Confederacy**. The Tuscarora join as a sixth nation in 1722.	English explorer Sir Francis Drake lands in California, where he meets the Miwok. The Miwok believed Drake and his men were gods of the sea. The explorers spent five weeks with the Miwok. Before he left, the Miwok crowned Drake their king.	Jamestown, Virginia, the first permanent English settlement in America, is founded.	Epidemics of smallpox, introduced by Europeans, kill 90 percent of Native Americans in the Massachusetts Bay region.

colonists needed land for farming and building. They were settling on Native American lands. British relations with the Native Americans often started out friendly. The Pilgrims at Plymouth, Massachusetts, for example, would not have survived their first winter without the help of the Pawtuxet (*paw-TUX-et*) Native American called **Squanto** (*SKWAN-toe*) (see p. 86). He taught them to plant crops in American soil. Pennsylvania founder **William Penn** (see p. 77) treated the Native Americans fairly. But almost everywhere, relations became worse. British colonists began to mistreat their Native American neighbors and take their land. Many wars between

French explorer Samuel de Champlain (center) founded Quebec City, the capital of New France. French explorers were generally on better terms with Native Americans than were English and Spanish colonists. (Library of Congress)

colonists and Native Americans were fought. Some of them include, in the Virginia colony, the Powhatan (*pow-HAT-un*) (see p. 44) Wars (see **Great Massacre** on p. 64); in New England, the **Pequot** (*PEE-kwat*) **War** (see p. 78); and in North Carolina, the **Tuscarora** (*tus-cuh-ROAR-uh*) **War** (see p. 89).

1620	**1622–1632**	**1632**	**1636–1637**
With the aid of local Native Americans, the Pilgrims, English colonists, found Plymouth, Massachusetts.	The Powhatan battle (see p. 44) the English colony of Virginia in the first of the Powhatan Wars. The second Powhatan War takes place from 1644 to 1646.	Peter Minuit, director general of **New Netherland**, buys Manhattan Island for $16 from local Native Americans.	In the **Pequot War**, the Pequot fight English settlers in Massachusetts and Connecticut and are defeated.

In New France, Native Americans did not always go unharmed from their alliance with the French. European *diseases* and alcohol plagued the Native nations. Native Americans fought in the European wars. They also fought among themselves over the European fur trade. One such conflict, called the Beaver Wars (see p. 58), destroyed the Huron.

Spain claimed a vast area of what is now the United States, including California, Arizona, New Mexico, Texas, and Florida. Spanish settlements grew slowly. Most Native Americans in these regions continued their old ways, with some changes. Native Americans living on the Great Plains, such as the Arapaho (*uh-RAP-uh-ho*) (see p. 23), Cheyenne (*shy-ANN*) (see p. 26), and Sioux (*soo*) (see p. 46), began using horses. The Spanish brought horses with them to the Americas. Horses dramatically changed the hunting methods of the Plains peoples, allowing them to take far more buffalo than ever before. However, Native Americans near Spanish settlements were forced to work and to convert to Christianity. Spanish abuses in Santa Fe, New Mexico, sparked the Pueblo Revolt (see p. 84). This revolt of Pueblo (see p. 44) peoples drove the Spanish out of the region for 12 years.

The Netherlands and Sweden both established North American colonies in the 17th century. These were called New Netherland (see p. 74) and New Sweden (see p. 76). By the end of the century, France and Great Britain had emerged as the most powerful imperial powers on the continent. They both fought for control of North America. Their struggle took the form

1649–1684

In the Beaver Wars, the Iroquois fight to expand their share of the beaver fur trade. The Iroquois grow in size and power by attacking the settlements of Native American allies of the French.

1664

The English conquer New Netherland and rename it New York, taking over its trading and military alliance with the Iroquois. The Dutch city of New Amsterdam becomes New York City.

1675–1676

In Bacon's Rebellion, Virginia settlers, angry at Native American raids, massacre Native Americans and revolt against the colonial government. Meanwhile, in Massachusetts, the Wampanoag fight colonists in King Philip's War, and are defeated.

1680

In the Pueblo Revolt, the Pueblo rise against Spanish rule in New Mexico, forcing the Spanish out of Santa Fe until 1692.

of four conflicts called the **French and Indian Wars** (see p. 62). These wars were named King William's War, Queen Anne's War, King George's War, and the **French and Indian War** (see p. 61). The French and British involved Native Americans as partners in all of these wars. Nations such as those in the **Iroquois** *(EAR-uh-kwoy)* **Confederacy** (see p. 66) allied with the British, and the **Abenaki** *(ah-buh-NA-kee)* (see p. 21) allied with the French. They became well known for raids they made on British and French settlements. Native Americans also took part in battles between French and British armies.

In the end, Great Britain won the control of North America. With the Peace of Paris in 1763, France surrendered most of its North American empire. Great Britain now claimed the land from Canada to the Gulf of Mexico, and from the Atlantic Ocean to the Mississippi River. France's Native American allies rebelled against the British. The revolt was called **Pontiac's Rebellion** (see p. 80).

The British defeated the revolt. They learned, however, that they had to maintain some fairness in their relations with Native Americans. They tried to do so with the **Proclamation of 1763** (see p. 83). The proclamation banned new settlements by American colonists in lands west of the Appalachian Mountains.

But for the Native Americans in those regions, great changes were also coming. A new nation, the United States, was about to be born, and it would renew the clash of worlds.

1689–1697	1702–1713	1711–1713	1729
King William's War is the first of four **French and Indian Wars** in which the British and their Native American allies clash with the French and their Native American allies for control of North America.	Queen Anne's War is the second of the **French and Indian Wars**. In the course of it, in 1704, French and Native American forces kill 50 English colonists and capture 100 in a massacre at Deerfield, Massachusetts.	In the **Tuscarora War**, the Tuscarora clash with English settlers in North Carolina and are defeated.	In Louisiana, the **Natchez** rebel against the French, who respond by destroying their society.

European Colonies in North America, 1754

The map below shows British, French, and Spanish territory in North America before the start of the French and Indian War. When the war ended in 1763, Britain had gained control of New France.

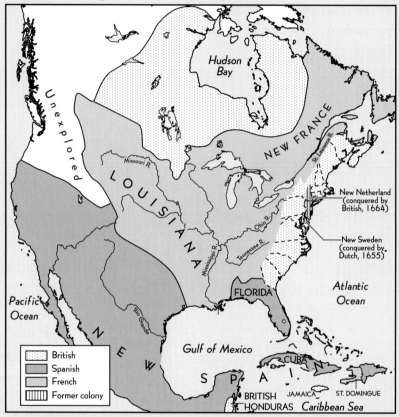

Key
British
Spanish
French
Former colony

1754–1763

The **French and Indian War** brings about the end of New France. France's Native American allies must now deal with the British as North America's dominant power.

1760–1761

The **Cherokee War** between the Cherokee and South Carolina colonists takes place. The war ends with the Cherokee being pushed further west.

1763

Britain issues the **Proclamation of 1763**, forbidding colonial expansion into Native American lands west of the Appalachian Mountains.

1763–1766

In **Pontiac's Rebellion**, in the Great Lakes region, Ottawa chief Pontiac leads Native Americans against British forces.

A-Z of Key People, Events, and Terms

Aztec Empire, Spanish conquest of

Spanish conquest of the Aztec Empire in Mesoamerica (*MEZ-oh-America*). During the Spanish exploration of Panama and the Yucatán Peninsula, the Spanish learned of the Aztec Empire to the north. This empire of 5 million people stretched from present-day Mexico and Guatemala to Salvador and Honduras. Its capital was Tenochtitlán (*tay-notch-teet-LAHN*), today's Mexico City. Hernán Cortés invaded the Aztec region with a force of 400 men. There was much unrest among other Mesoamerican nations the Aztecs had conquered. Another advantage Cortés had was the fear the Native Americans had of his guns and horses. Native Americans had never seen either.

The Aztecs drove the Spanish out of the city. In August 1521, Cortés returned and retook Tenochtitlán. He tried to erase all traces of the Aztec Empire. He burned books, destroyed temples, and forced the Aztecs to work for the Spanish. Despite the destruction of the empire, Aztec ways continue to influence Mexican culture.

Bacon's Rebellion

A series of attacks on Native Americans in 1675–1676. A dispute over an unpaid debt led to an attack on the Nanticoke (*NANT-ih-coke*) and Susquehannock (*sus-kwa-HAHN-ock*) nations by colonists in Maryland and Virginia. The Native Americans then attacked the colonists' settlements.

Nathaniel Bacon was a cousin of Virginia governor Sir William Berkeley. Bacon formed a group who attacked not only the Susquehannock but also several peaceful Native American nations, including the **Powhatan Confederacy** (see p. 44). When Governor Berkeley named Bacon a traitor and rebel, Bacon returned to Jamestown and destroyed it. He died shortly afterward and the rebellion was ended. However, the rebellion he led had set a pattern. Settlers would repeat the use of a dispute with one Native American nation as an excuse to attack others.

In 1675, a group of Virginia and Maryland colonists, led by Nathaniel Bacon, attacked and killed members of the Nanticoke, Susquehannock, and other nations following a dispute with the Nanticoke. Bacon then attacked and briefly captured Jamestown, the colony's capital. He is shown here confronting the governor of Virginia. (Library of Congress)

Beaver Wars

Struggle between the **Iroquois Confederacy** (see p. 66) and other Native Americans for control of the beaver fur trade lasting from 1649 to 1684. The Huron and their allies started a profitable business gathering beaver pelts from a wide territory. They sold the furs to the French in what is now Canada. The Iroquois, who were allied with the Dutch, wanted to capture some of the Huron/French territory and its rich trade. The result was a series of raids and wars. The Iroquois attacked the Huron and destroyed them. From then on, the Iroquois attacked Native American nations, such as the **Miami** (see p. 38), with which the Huron had traded. The Iroquois dominated the fur trade in a region that stretched from present-day Canada to Kentucky. In 1684, the Illinois Confederacy, other Native American nations, and their French allies defeated the Iroquois at Fort St. Louis on the Illinois River.

Cherokee War

Conflict between Native Americans and colonists in South Carolina in 1760 and 1761. The **Cherokee** (see p. 25) fought with the British against the French in the **French and Indian War** (see p. 61). Later, the British killed several Cherokee in a dispute over horses. The Cherokee responded by raiding British settlements and forts. The British destroyed Cherokee towns and crops. Finally, the Cherokee surrendered, giving up their land and retreating further away from British settlements.

Columbian exchange

The passing of biological species between the Old World and the New World. These two worlds were in separate parts of the globe. Each had developed very different animals, plants, and even *diseases*. The explorations of **Christopher Columbus** (see p. 60) began contact between the worlds. Each received from the other food crops, livestock, and diseases it had not previously known.

European diseases were especially harmful to Native Americans. They lacked a natural immunity to, or ability to fight off, the diseases. Native Americans died in great numbers from diseases such as smallpox, influenza, measles, malaria, typhus, and diphtheria. In Mexico, the estimated Native American population of 25 million in 1519 dropped to 1 million by the 1620s.

Smallpox epidemics killed 90 percent of Native Americans in the Massachusetts Bay region. Similar waves of disease occurred throughout the Americas. Syphilis, a sexually transmitted disease, is believed to have been passed from the Americas to Europe. The illness was brought to Europe by crewmembers on Columbus's first expedition.

Native Americans had few farm animals before the Europeans arrived. The Europeans brought with them horses, cows, sheep, goats, pigs, chickens, and donkeys. One kind of Native American animal was the guinea pig. Native Americans in South America raised it for food. The Columbian exchange introduced it around the world. It later became known as a pet and laboratory animal.

Along with the good species came the bad. Weeds and vermin were mistakenly shipped across the ocean. These included New World dandelions and Old World rats. Some Native Americans before Columbus had known alcohol. However, most obtained alcohol in trade with Europeans. Substances such as tobacco and coca, the source of cocaine, were passed from the New World to the Old World.

Disease in the New World

English scientist Thomas Harriot took part in the first attempt to colonize Roanoke Island, North Carolina (1585–1586). There he saw an occurrence that would be repeated throughout the Western Hemisphere: wherever Europeans set foot, Native Americans got sick and died. Harriot believed the Indians' illness was God's punishment for wickedness.

[W]ithin a few days after our departure from every . . . town, the people began to die very fast, and many in short space, in some towns about twenty, in some forty, and in some [120], which in truth was very many in respect to their numbers. This happened in no place that we could learn but where we had been....The disease was also strange, that they neither knew what it was, nor how to cure it....All the space of their sickness, there was no man of ours known to die, or that was especially sick.

Source: Thomas Harriot, *A Briefe and True Report of the New Found Land of Virginia.*

Both parts of the globe gained new sources of food. Some of the many crops the Old and New Worlds exchanged were:

From the New World: avocado; cacao (source of chocolate); cashews; cranberry; maize (corn); peanut; potato; red pepper; squash; tomato.

From the Old World: apple; banana; coffee; grape; olive; orange; peach; rice; sugar; wheat.

Columbus, Christopher

Explorer and navigator. Columbus was born in 1451 in Genoa, Italy, and became a sailor at the age of 20. He looked for and was granted the support he needed from King Ferdinand and Queen Isabella of Spain. On August 3, 1492, Columbus set sail with three vessels, the *Nina*, *Pinta*, and *Santa Maria*. His goal was to reach the markets of the Far East. These markets, called the Indies, were located in present-day China and India. Columbus believed he would reach the Indies by sailing westward across the Atlantic Ocean. He reached the island now called San Salvador in the Bahamas. Natives, whom he called "Indians" in the mistaken belief that he had reached the Indies, greeted him. In fact they were the **Arawak** (see p. 23), a friendly, gentle people. Columbus quickly realized he could easily overpower and enslave the Arawak. Next, Columbus went to what are now Cuba and Hispaniola, present-day Haiti, and the Dominican Republic, to find gold. He brought gold and Arawak prisoners to Spain and presented them to Ferdinand and Isabella.

Columbus made three other journeys to the Caribbean. He explored the islands, searching for gold and enslaving Native Americans. Columbus agreed to have Native Americans killed if they resisted their enslavement.

Columbus opened the way for Europeans to a part of the world that had been unknown to them. He is credited as the European discoverer of the Americas. While Native Americans arrived in the Americas long before Columbus's "discovery," the voyages of Columbus were a turning point in the history of the world. For Europeans, the centuries that followed Columbus's voyages brought exploration and settlement. For Native Americans, Columbus's voyages would eventually bring an end to a way of life. Columbus died in 1506.

Deganawida (*deg-ahn-un-WE-duh*) Cofounder of the **Iroquois Confederacy** (see p. 66). In the early 1500s, five Native American nations occupied the area of today's upstate New York and Lake Ontario region. These nations—the Cayuga (*cay-YOO-guh*), Mohawk, Oneida (*ohn-EYE-duh*), Onondaga (*oh-nen-DAH-gah*), and Seneca, had long fought among themselves. Deganawida, also called the Peacemaker, was Huron. He had a vision of the united nations sheltering under a Tree of Great Peace. He won the support of **Hiawatha** (*hi-uh-WAH-thuh*) (see p. 65), a Mohawk who was a great speaker. Together the two persuaded the five nations to form a peaceful confederation. In 1570, they formed an alliance called the League of Five Nations, also known as the Iroquois Confederacy. The *confederacy* took its name from the Iroquois language they all spoke. The leaders of the five nations formed a democratic government. The Iroquois Confederacy inspired the founders of the United States.

French and Indian War

The last and most important in a series of four wars between Great Britain and France over control of land in North America. It lasted from 1754 to 1763. In Europe it was known as the Seven Years' War. France and Great Britain battled over each other's expansion across the Alleghenies and into the Ohio River valley. The French claimed the region that includes today's Canada and the land south along the Mississippi River to New Orleans. They saw the spread of British settlers as a threat and built forts along the upper Ohio.

The Log of Christopher Columbus

On Friday, October 12, 1492, Italian mariner Christopher Columbus landed in the Bahamas. After claiming them for Spain, he made contact with the Arawak people. In his log, Columbus described them with both admiration and insensitivity, as he looked ahead to their usefulness as servants.

No sooner had we [taken] the island than people began to come to the beach, all as naked as their mothers bore them . . . I showed my one sword, and through ignorance he grabbed it by the blade and cut himself. . . . I want the natives to develop a friendly attitude toward us because I know that they are a people who can be made free and converted to our Holy Faith more by love than by force. I therefore gave red caps to some and glass beads to others. They hung the beads around their necks, along with some other things of slight value that I gave them. And they took great pleasure in this and became so friendly that it was a marvel. . .They ought to make good and skilled servants.

Source: *The Log of Chistopher Columbus' First Voyage to America in the Year 1492.*

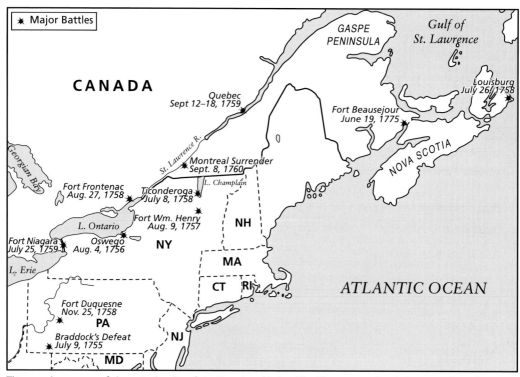

This map shows many of the major battles of the French and Indian War. The war was fought between Great Britain and France for control of American land. Some Native Americans fought with the British, and others fought with the French.

Most Native American nations were allied with the French. They realized the French were interested only in trade and furs. The British colonists wanted Native American land. Many native nations raided British settlements and joined the French in battle against the British. In 1755, British General Edward Braddock suffered a major defeat near Fort Duquesne (*du-KAYNE*), modern-day Pittsburgh, by French soldiers and **Huron** (see p. 34) and Potawatomi (*poh-tuh-WAH-tow-mi*) warriors. The results were twofold: Nearly all Native American nations joined the French, and the new British settlements became exposed to attack.

For two years the war went badly for the British. Then, in 1758, British General James Wolfe took Quebec. Montreal was taken the following year. The French gave up their claims to Canada and the Mississippi Valley in the Peace of Paris of 1763.

French and Indian Wars

A series of four wars in North America from the late 17th to the mid-18th century. Each of the wars reflected the struggle for

British and Colonial American Treaties with Native Americans, 1754–1763

During the French and Indian War, representatives of Great Britain and many of the American colonies made treaties with Native Americans. In most treaties, Native Americans agreed to land *cessions*, or to give up land.

Date	Parties	Provisions
July 11, 1754	Iroquois-Pennsylvania	land cession
Aug. 29, 1754	Catawba-North Carolina	friendship, land cession
Dec. 17, 1754	Iroquois-Great Britain	land cession
Nov. 24, 1755	Cherokee-Great Britain	land cession
Dec. 1755	Creek-Georgia	friendship
Apr. 1–May 22, 1757	Iroquois, Delaware, Nanticoke Susquehannock-Pennsylvania	alliance
Apr. 1757	Mahican, Shawnee, Nanticoke-Great Britain	friendship
Dec. 21-28, 1759	Cherokee-North Carolina	peace, resumption of trade
Aug. 12, 1760	Iroquois–Great Britain	friendship
Dec. 17, 1761	Cherokee-Great Britain	peace/boundary line/return of prisoners
Nov. 5, 1763	Cherokee, Creek, Choctaw, Chickasaw-Great Britain	boundary definition, peace, land cession

dominance in Europe among the three major powers: France, Spain, and Great Britain.

King William's War (1689–1697) began with battles between Great Britain and France over the Rhineland in present-day Germany. In North America, the French and British forces fought in Hudson Bay. Native American allies of the French joined them in raids. These raids devastated areas of Maine and New Hampshire.

Queen Anne's War (1702–1713) was known as the War of the Spanish Succession in Europe. In this European war, France and Spain were allies. In North America, Spanish forces fought to keep the southern region of the Mississippi River free of French fur traders. Meanwhile, the French attacked Great Britain's New England colonies. The Treaty of Utrecht (*YOU-trekt*) ended the war. It recognized Great Britain's claim to Hudson Bay and Nova Scotia, Canada.

King George's War (1744–1748) was known as the War of the Austrian Succession in Europe. In North America, there were raids into New England from Canada and an attack on Cape Breton Island from Nova Scotia.

The **French and Indian War** (1754–1763) (see p. 61) was known in Europe as the Seven Years' War. The French traders had increased the prices of goods they sold to the Native Americans. The native nations began to ally with the British. After the defeat of British General Edward Braddock at Fort Duquesne, many went back to ally with the French.

In all four wars, most Native American nations in the North allied with the French. These included the **Abenaki** (see p. 21), **Ojibwa** (*oh-JIB-way*) (see p. 41), and Ottawa. The **Iroquois Confederacy** (see p. 66) fought with the British in King William's War. The French defeated them, and they agreed that they would remain neutral in future wars.

The wars were in some ways helpful to Native Americans. Both French and British forces needed their support as allies. This increased their power to gain territory and win trade goods and other rewards. In other ways, the Native Americans suffered great losses. They died in battles, had their villages destroyed, and realized a general increase in brutality. For example, both the French and British paid bounties for the scalps of their enemies. This made the unusual practice of scalping enemies common during these wars.

At the end of the final war (1763), France was forced to give up most of its North American empire. This also ended the chance for Native Americans to gain any favors from either the French or the British.

Great Massacre

Slaughter of English colonists by the **Powhatan Confederacy** (see p. 44) in 1622. There were disputes between the Virginia

Company, made of the Jamestown settlers, and the Powhatan over the land the settlers claimed. Settlers needed it to grow tobacco, which had become popular in Europe. Powhatan chief **Opechancanough** (*oh-puh-CAN-cuh-naw*) (see p. 77) decided to stop this constant expansion. He attacked Jamestown and killed 346 men, women, and children. This loss of life represented nearly a third of the English population of Virginia. The attack brought the Virginia Company to an end. However, it did not stop British expansion. A royal charter replaced the company, and settlers organized a militia force. Regular patrols were sent against Native Americans, whose crops were destroyed. The Powhatan Wars continued.

Hendrick (Tiyanoga the Great)

Mohawk chief (ca. 1680–1755). A supporter of the British, he toured London. He was friendly with **Sir William Johnson** (see p. 67), British superintendent for Indian affairs. During the **French and Indian War** (see p. 61), Hendrick led Mohawk troops. They fought alongside Johnson in the Battle of Lake George. Though Hendrick was killed, the Mohawks helped secure a British victory in the battle.

Hiawatha (*hi-uh-WAH-thuh*)

Mohawk medicine man. Hiawatha was a great speaker and a student of the **Huron** (see p. 34) **Deganawida** (see p. 61). Together, the two helped form the League of Five Nations, or **Iroquois Confederacy** (see p. 66). Hiawatha preached to the Cayuga, Mohawk, Onondaga, Oneida, and Seneca nations. He taught them to understand how ending their intertribal warfare would be helpful. He believed that political and military unity would bring the confederacy power and influence. Over the next 100 years, the Five Nations became the greatest Native American military power in North

Over 300 years after his death, Hiawatha became the subject of a famous poem by Henry Wadsworth Longfellow called "The Song of Hiawatha." This illustration shows Hiawatha with his fictional love, Minnehaha. Longfellow's poem was based on an Ojibwa legend, not on the real life of Hiawatha, who was a Mohawk. (Library of Congress)

America. It remained an important political force until the American Revolution.

Inca Empire, fall of

Spanish conquest of the Inca civilization. Ten years after Hernán Cortés conquered the **Aztec** (see p. 24) Empire, Francisco Pizarro explored the Pacific coastline of South America. He had heard there was an empire there that was richer than that of the Aztecs. He took his force inland to the city of Caxamalca (*kaks-uh-MAL-cuh*), today's Caxamarca (*kaks-uh-MAR-cuh*), Peru. He met the Inca leader Atahualpa (*at-uh-WAL-puh*), who greeted him peacefully. Atahualpa was killed, and Pizarro went on to capture more cities. By 1537, his destruction of the Inca Empire was complete.

Iroquois Confederacy

One of the earliest drawings of an Iroquois, by a French fur trapper, around 1700. (New York Public Library Picture Collection)

Alliance of Native American nations. Based in what is now upstate New York, the confederacy had five original member nations. These nations were the Cayuga, Mohawk, Oneida, Onondaga, and Seneca. These hunting and farming nations developed a tradition that became distinctive to the Iroquois. The tradition was the use of *longhouses*, bark-covered structures that housed many families and served as meeting places.

In the 16th century, the five nations banded together to form the Iroquois Confederacy, or League of Five Nations. According to tradition, Deganawida and Hiawatha founded the league. Each nation governed its own affairs, and maintained peace with fellow nations. Issues affecting one or more of the nations were decided through a ruling council. The council was made up of delegates from each nation. The delegates were chiefs and were selected by female leaders from each nation. The confederacy had a democratic structure with a constitution. This constitution was used to help the confederacy govern its members. The confederacy's constitution influenced the development of the U.S. Constitution. At its height, the confederacy may have numbered 25,000 people.

The Tuscarora, from North Carolina, joined the Iroquois Confederacy in 1722. The confederacy was now the League of Six Nations. The Iroquois Confederacy split during the American Revolution (1775–1783). This split was caused when four

Constitution of the Iroquois Confederacy

The Iroquois Confederacy, an alliance of five Native American nations, was founded in New York in about 1570. It governed itself through a constitution that was originally spoken, instead of written down. The balanced, democratic structure of the Iroquois central government influenced the framers of the U.S. Constitution. In the 19th century, the Iroquois Constitution was put into writing in several versions. This is the opening of one, written in 1880.

This is the wisdom and justice of the part of the Great Spirit, to create and raise chiefs, give and establish unchangeable laws, rules and customs between the Five Nation Indians, viz the Mohawks, Oneidas, Onondagas, Cayugas, and Senecas and the other nations of Indians here in North America. The object of these laws is to establish peace between the numerous nations of Indians, hostility will be done away with, for the preservation and protection of life, property, and liberty.

Laws, rules and customs as follows:

And the number of chiefs in this confederation of the Five Nation Indians are 50 in number, no more and no less. They are the ones to arrange, to legislate, and to look after the affairs of their people.

[T]he Mohawks . . . and their representatives in this confederation is nine chiefs. . .And the Oneidas . . . and their representatives in this confederation is nine chiefs. . .And the Onondagas. . . and their representatives in this confederation is fourteen chiefs.. . .And the Cayugas . . . and their representatives in this confederation is ten chiefs. . . And the Senecas . . . and their representatives in this confederation is eight chiefs.

And when the . . . chiefs assemble to hold a council, the council shall be duly opened and closed by the Onondaga chiefs, the Firekeepers. They will offer thanks to the Great Spirit that dwells in heaven above: the source and ruler of our lives, and it is him that sends daily blessings upon us, our daily wants and daily health, and they will then declare the council open for the . . . business.

Source: *The Constitution of the Five Nations*, or *The Iroquois Book of the Great Law.*

nations sided with the British, and two sided with the Americans. The Iroquois Confederacy was later revived, but never regained its former strength.

Johnson, Sir William

Superintendent of Indian affairs. Born in Great Britain, Johnson arrived in America and bought land in the Mohawk River valley in present-day New York. He traded with the **Iroquois Confederacy** (see p. 66) and earned their trust. The confederacy requested that the British appoint Johnson as agent for Indian affairs. Although loyal to the British crown, Johnson did much to help the Native Americans. He brought about the Treaty of Fort Stanwix (*STAN-wicks*). He hoped this treaty

The Captivity of Mary Rowlandson

King Philip's War (1675–1676), an uprising of Native Americans in New England, brought death and suffering to both colonists and Indians. It also inspired a new and popular kind of writing: firsthand accounts of white settlers taken captive by Native Americans. The first was that of Mary Rowlandson, published in 1682 as *The Sovereignty and Goodness of God*. In this passage, she recounts her capture in a raid on the frontier town of Lancaster, Massachusetts, in February 1676. She was ransomed and freed three months later.

On the tenth of February, 1676, Came the Indians with great numbers upon Lancaster: Their first coming was about Sun-rising; hearing the noise of some Guns, we looked out; several Houses were burning, and the Smoke ascending to Heaven....

At length they came and beset our own house, and quickly it was the dolefullest [saddest] day that ever mine eyes saw....Then I took my Children (and one of my sisters, hers) to go forth and leave the house: but as soon as we came to the [door]

and appeared, the Indians shot so thick that the bullets rattled against the House. . . . But out we must go, the fire increasing, and coming along behind us, roaring, and the Indians gaping before us with their Guns, Spears, and Hatchets to devour us. No sooner were we out of the House, but my Brother in Law . . . fell down dead, wherat the Indians scornfully shouted, and hallowed, and were presently upon him, stripping off his cloths, the bullets flying thick, one went through my side, and the same (as would seem) through the bowels and hand of dear Child in my arms. One of my elder Sisters Children, named William, had then his leg broken, which the Indians, perceiving, they knockt him on the head. ...The Indians laid hold of us, pulling me one way, and the Children another, and said, Come go along with us; I told them they would kill me: they answered, If I were willing to go along with them, they would not hurt me....Now away we must go with those Barbarous Creatures, with our bodies wounded and bleeding, and our hearts no less than our bodies.

Source: Mary Rowlandson, *The Sovereignty and Goodness of God*.

During King Philip's War, Native Americans often made successful surprise attacks against colonists, but in the end, the Native Americans were no match for the weapons carried by the colonists. (Library of Congress)

would settle the boundaries between the colonies and Native American land.

King Philip's War

Native American uprising in 1675 and 1676 against the colonists of Massachusetts and Rhode Island. Metacomet (*met-uh-CAHM-et*) (1636?–1676), the **Wampanoag** (*wam-puh-NOH-ag*) (see p. 48) chief, had maintained peaceful relations with the colonists. Conflicts arose as the colonists continued to settle on and claim Wampanoag lands. Metacomet attacked the settlement of Swansea on Narragansett Bay. During the next few months, an alliance of five nations—Wampanoag, Nipmuck (*NIP-muk*), Narragansett, Mohegan, and Podunk—attacked 52 settlements in Massachusetts and Rhode Island. Twelve of the settlements were completely destroyed.

The remaining colonists organized armed forces. They fought and defeated each of the five nations. The final attack was led against Metacomet at Mount Hope on Narragansett Bay. Within 20 years, the New England settlements that had been destroyed were restored.

Massasoit (*MASS-uh-soyt*)

Wampanoag (see p. 48) chief. When the English Pilgrims arrived in North America, Massasoit sent his people to help the newcomers plant crops and build huts. He invited the Pilgrims to join his nation's annual harvest ceremony. This ceremony has become the basis for our modern Thanksgiving holiday.

Later, he prepared a formal peace treaty with the settlers. In the treaty, each side pledged to help the other in times of war.

The peace treaty established practices that were based on English customs. The settlers believed that when they bought land from the Wampanoag, it became their private property. The Native Americans did not understand the concept of private ownership. They believed the English payments were a form of rent to hunt or farm the land. They didn't understand why they could no longer use the land themselves after it had been sold.

The Wampanoag tried to maintain friendly relations with the settlers and never broke the treaty. By the time Massasoit died, 35,000 settlers had come to New England.

missionaries

Europeans who came to the New World to convert Native Americans to Christianity. The missionaries built churches and schools in the Americas. They wanted to teach the native people

A Spanish mission in Santa Fe, New Mexico. (Library of Congress)

about Christ and to help them adopt European culture. Both Catholics and Protestants believed the souls of Native Americans could be saved only if they became Christians and gave up their traditional ways.

Catholic missionaries were part of Spain's exploration and colonization effort in the Americas. It required that conquered Native Americans be converted to Christianity. The Spanish welcomed the help of all missionaries. The missionaries belonged to various religious orders, including the Franciscans, Dominicans, and Jesuits. Franciscans were especially common in Mexico. The Spanish missionary Bartolomé de Las Casas told of the abusive treatment of Native Americans in the **West Indies** (see p. 89) and fought to help them. The Italian-born Jesuit priest Eusebio (*yoo-SAY-bee-oh*) Kino founded missions among several Native American nations in what is now Arizona.

French Jesuit missionaries were among those who worked to convert Indians to Christianity. (Library of Congress)

Spanish missionaries founded chains of missions in Florida, Texas, New Mexico, and California. The missions taught Christianity and provided food, shelter, and protection to those who wanted them. However, many missionaries separated Native Americans from their people and forced them to work. Native Americans resented giving up their religions and customs. In the **Pueblo Revolt** (see p. 84), the Spanish missionaries and settlers were temporarily driven out of Santa Fe, New Mexico. The revolt was, in part, over religious conflict.

The French allowed Catholic Jesuit missionaries into their territories through their early trading posts. The Jesuits attempted to convert the **Huron** (see p. 34). However, a smallpox outbreak spread throughout the Huron peoples and killed many. The tribes of the **Iroquois Confederacy** (see p. 66) took this opportunity to defeat the remaining Huron, and the Jesuits left the region.

The English Protestants were also active in trying to convert the Native Americans. Puritan John Eliot (1604–1690) established

"Praying Villages" for Native Americans. The first was in Natick, Massachusetts. Large numbers of Native Americans were stricken with *diseases* brought from Europe. Those who did not die often joined the Praying Villages to survive. Known as the "Apostle to the Indians," Eliot translated the Bible into Algonquian.

Some of the conversion efforts by the Europeans succeeded, but many did not. Today, many Native Americans continue to practice some form of their traditional religions. Others have blended Christian and traditional elements into new varieties of belief and ritual.

Some missionaries were helpful to the Native Americans. They provided different Native nations with a common language, offered ways for the nations to work together, and gave them an understanding of European culture. This would later help the Native Americans in dealings with non-Indian governments. But the missionaries also spread fatal diseases and, most times, forced or tricked Native Americans into changing their religions and cultures.

Neolin (*NEE-oh-lin*)

Native American prophet called "The Imposter" by the British. A **Delaware** (see p. 30) named Neolin, which means "enlightened one," became well known. The Native Americans called him the Delaware Prophet of Ohio. A great speaker, Neolin preached about the need to return to old Native American customs. He taught that Native Americans should not use firearms. He also preached that the Native American nations should join forces against European settlement. He believed that Native Americans would be restored to their previous wealth and positions only after the Europeans were driven out of America.

Neolin's preaching came at a time when the British had taken Quebec and Montreal and had defeated the French in Canada. The native peoples around the Great Lakes had supported the French. They found the British settlers and soldiers were not concerned with Native American rights and customs. They agreed with everything that Neolin was preaching. The result led to **Pontiac's Rebellion** (see p. 80).

Strange Goods

On their first encounter with European trade goods, Native Americans were not always sure how to use them. In this excerpt, Waioskasit (*wy-oh-SKA-sit*), a Menominee, remembers his people's first contact with French traders. The meeting probably took place in the 1660s, on the shore of a "sea" that is probably Lake Michigan. The encounter introduced the Menominee to alcohol, flour, guns, and kettles.

When the Menominee lived on the shore of the sea, they one day were looking out across the water and observed some large vessels. . . . Suddenly there was a terrific explosion, as of thunder, which startled the people greatly.

When the vessels approached . . . men with light-colored skin landed. Most . . . had hair on their faces, and . . . carried . . . heavy sticks ornamented with shining metal. As the strangers came toward the Indians, the latter believed the leader to be a great manido [spirit], with his companions. . . .

Then some of the strangers brought . . . some parcels which contained a liquid, of which they drank, finally offering some to the Menominee. The Indians, however, were afraid to drink . . . fearing it would kill them; therefore four useless old men were selected to drink the liquor, and thus to be experimented on, that it might be found whether the liquor would kill them . . .

The men drank the liquid, and although they had previously been very silent and gloomy, they now began to talk and to grow amused. . . .

The chief of the strangers next gave the Indians some flour, but they did not know what to do with it. The white chief then showed the Indians some biscuits, and told them how they were baked. When that was over, one of the white men presented to an Indian a gun, after firing it to show how far away anything could be killed. The Indian was afraid to shoot it, fearing the gun would knock him over. . . .

Source: "Thunder, Dizzying Liquid, and Cups That Do Not Grow," in Peter Nabokov, ed., *Native American Testimony.*

New France

The name given to French colonies in North America. New France began in 1535 as a series of trading posts on Cape Breton Island off Canada's east coast. By 1608, Samuel de Champlain had founded Quebec. Other French settlements were beginning to appear along the St. Lawrence River. In 1682, René Robert de La Salle traveled the Mississippi River to its mouth. He claimed for France the territory later called Louisiana.

The French attracted few farming settlers to their American territories. The basis for New France's economy was the beaver fur trade. This trading took place through a network of forts and trading posts. Because the French relied on Native Americans to trap beavers and collect their furs, they treated them with respect and generosity. The success of New France rested on its trade and military alliances with a number of Native American nations. Among these nations were the Huron. The French and their Native American allies joined in fighting against the Iroquois in the **Beaver Wars** (see p. 58) and against the British in the **French and Indian Wars** (see p. 62). French missionaries were active in North America, but they were not successful at forcing Native Americans to convert to Christianity.

The French did not always live peacefully with the Native Americans. For example, in 1729, they defeated an uprising of the **Natchez** (*NATCH-ez*) (see p. 40) in the lower Mississippi River valley. The French destroyed the nation. Other nations took in most survivors. Some were enslaved and sold.

New France came to an end in 1763, when Great Britain conquered it in the **French and Indian War** (see p. 61).

New Netherland

Dutch colony in the Hudson Valley of modern-day New York State from 1624 to 1667. This Dutch settlement in North America began with the journey of Henry Hudson. He was an English explorer who was employed by the Netherlands. Hudson sailed up the Hudson River in 1609 as far as today's Albany, New York. In 1621 the Dutch West India Company was formed, sending its first colonists to the New World. Cornelis Mey, the first governor of New Netherland, arrived with 30 families, who settled a large stretch of the Hudson Valley area. In 1626, Peter Minuit arrived and bargained with Native Americans to purchase the island of Manhattan. In exchange for the island that is now the center of New York City, he gave the Native Americans goods worth approximately $16 in today's money. Fort Amsterdam was built shortly thereafter, and the island became New Amsterdam. Minuit served as the colony's governor.

New Netherland was a successful trading center for fur but it attracted few farming settlers. Beginning in 1629, some estates

Native Americans peer out over what will later be renamed the Hudson River, as they watch Henry Hudson's ship, the *Half Moon*, appear in the distance. (Library of Congress)

were granted to those who brought settlers from Europe. This practice was known as *patroonship*. The increased demand for land and cruel treatment of the Native Americans worsened relations with Native Americans. For example, during the conflict between Dutch and Native Americans called Kieft's (*keefts*) War, Governor Willem Kieft encouraged a Dutch and Mohawk massacre of Wappinger (*WOP-in-jur*) men, women, and children. Native American raids during that war forced the Dutch to retreat to what is now southern Manhattan. There, they built a defensive wall at the location of present-day Wall Street. Another conflict was the Peach War. This conflict started when a Dutch farmer killed a **Delaware** (see p. 30) woman for picking peaches on his land.

New Netherland annexed the colony of **New Sweden** (see p. 76) in 1655. In 1664, New Netherland was itself conquered by English forces. The colony's population was only half Dutch, due to European immigration. It was awarded to England in 1667 by the Peace of Breda. New Netherland became the provinces of New York and New Jersey, and New Amsterdam became the city of New York.

Swedish settlers mingle with members of the Delaware Nation in this 20th-century tribute to New Sweden. (Library of Congress)

New Sweden

Small, short-lived Swedish-Finnish colony in present-day Delaware. The Swedish West India Company established the colony of New Sweden in 1638. One of the colony's founders was Peter Minuit, previously a governor of **New Netherland** (see p. 74). Minuit sailed up the Delaware River and bought some land from the native Lenápe, or **Delaware** (see p. 30). There, he built Fort Christina, today's Wilmington, Delaware. New Sweden claimed about 50 miles of land along the banks of the Delaware and settled only about 200–300 Swedes and Finns. In 1643, its capital became Tinicum (*TIN-ih-cum*) Island, near Philadelphia. New Sweden's governors wanted to keep what little authority they had. They refused to allow traders from New Amsterdam, today's New York, to trade in Delaware Bay. This action caused the governor of New Amsterdam, Peter Stuyvesant *(STY-vuh-sunt)*, to take over the colony in 1655.

After New Sweden was *annexed*, many of the settlers moved west to the area that was to become Philadelphia. They established farms there and provided food for **William Penn**'s (see p. 77) first settlers, who arrived 30 years later. Penn's charter for land in the New World would include the Delaware region that once was New Sweden.

Opechancanough (*oh-puh-CAN-cuh-naw*)

Pamunkey (*PAHM-un-key*) chieftain. Opechancanough took over the leadership of the **Powhatan Confederacy** (see p. 44) from his brother, Chief **Powhatan** (see p. 83). His move to power began 25 years of hostilities between his people and the English colonists of Virginia. The colonists had claimed Native American lands to grow tobacco. Opechancanough and his followers attacked the colonists at the settlement of Jamestown. Over a third of the colonists were killed and Jamestown was destroyed. The uprising lasted for 10 years before an uneasy peace was restored. By that time warfare and *disease* had reduced the Powhatan. Opechancanough led a second uprising against the Virginia colony. Fighting continued for two years before he was captured and killed in Jamestown.

The wars in which Opechancanough was a leader are sometimes called the Powhatan Wars.

Paxton Boys

Colonial vigilantes. The Paxton Riots took place in 1763–1764. A group of colonists from Paxton, Pennsylvania, pledged to kill any Native Americans they found. The group was angry at all Native Americans because some had attacked colonial settlements. The Paxton Boys, as they were known, first murdered a group of Susquehannock and other Native Americans at the Conestoga Moravian Mission. Called Moravian Indians or Conestoga Mission Indians by the settlers, they were converts to Christianity who had settled on a reservation. The Paxton Boys went on to kill other Moravian Indians and vowed to kill more. When the Pennsylvania governor publicly condemned the attacks, the Paxton Boys marched on Philadelphia. They threatened to kill Native Americans in the city. Benjamin Franklin negotiated an agreement to stop the riots. The state government agreed to protect the frontier and to pay a *bounty* for the scalps of hostile Native Americans.

Penn, William

Founder of Pennsylvania. The son of a British admiral, William Penn became a Quaker as a young man. When the Quakers secured land in North America, Penn wrote the settlement's charter of

The Petition of the Pequot

In the Pequot War (1636–1637), most of the Pequot of Connecticut were killed or forced to leave. In 1655, some were resettled near New Haven. As the colonial population grew, English settlers began to move onto Pequot land. In 1735, they petitioned Governor Joseph Talcott for help. Help never came, but their petition leaves a record of what it was like to have one's land invaded in small steps.

To the Honble. Joseph Talcott, Esqr. Groton [Connecticut], Sept. 22, 1735. Honorable and worthy Sir Gover Talcott Sir after our humble Respects to your honor these are to inform your Self of the wrongs and distress that we me[et] with by Some People that make possessions of our land. They destroy so much of our timber for fencing and for other uses that we sha[nt] . . . have enough for fire wood . . . [B]y fencing in . . . our land they take away . . . our orchards for they let their own swine [pigs] go in and eat up our apples . . . and if our swine accidently get in they commit them to the pound . . . We see plainly that their chiefest desire is to deprive us of . . . our land, and drive us to our utter ruin . . . [I]t makes us concerned for our Children . . . what will become of them . . .

Source: Connecticut State Library.

self-government. He traveled to America with grants of land received from King Charles II and from the Duke of York. The land grants were located north of present-day Maryland. He agreed to a treaty of friendship with the Delaware Nation. It was the first such treaty signed by Native Americans. Penn came to a similar agreement with the Susquehannock (*sus-kwa-HAHN-uck*). He earned the trust of the Native Americans by making every effort to protect their rights and respect their religious beliefs. As a result, the colony of Pennsylvania enjoyed many peaceful years.

Pequot War

First major conflict in New England between Native Americans and British colonists. The **Pequot** (see p. 43) controlled most of the coastal area from the Connecticut River to Rhode Island. Their chief, Sassacus (*SASS-uh-cus*), resented the demands of English settlers for land. Disputes also arose over trade goods. The Pequot were suspected of killing a European trader. The Massachusetts Bay Colony sent a force of men under John Endecott to take

Ætatis suæ 21 A°.1616.

Matoaks als Rebecka daughter to the mighty Prince
Powhatan Emperour of Attanovghkomouck als Virgin
converted and baptized in the Chriftian faith an
Wife to the wor.ll Mr Tho: Rolff.

Pocahontas, in a formal portrait painted in England, following her marriage to Englishman John Rolfe. (Library of Congress)

revenge. They burned several Pequot and Narragansett (*narr-uh-GAN-set*) villages.

Sassacus later attacked Fort Saybrook at the mouth of the Connecticut River and raided outlying settlements. The colonists, allied with the Mohegan, Niantic, and Narragansett nations, formed an army. Between 1636 and 1637, this force attacked Sassacus's village and killed nearly 1,000 Pequot. Those Pequot taken alive were enslaved and sold. The few who escaped went to join other Algonquian nations in Long Island and Massachusetts.

Pocahontas

Powhatan (see p. 44) woman. Pocahontas (1595–1617) was the daughter of Powhatan, the chief of the Powhatan

Representatives of the Ottawa nation meet with British commanders to negotiate surrender in 1766, ending Pontiac's Rebellion. (Library of Congress)

Confederacy. The Powhatan lived in Virginia around Jamestown. In 1608, they took several colonists, including John Smith, prisoner for claiming Powhatan land. There is a legend that Pocahontas bargained with her father to save Smith's life. Whether this is true or not, Chief Powhatan did release Smith unharmed. In 1613, Pocahontas was captured by the British settlers and held as a hostage in Jamestown. She was well treated and converted to Christianity. In 1614, with her father's agreement, she married colonist John Rolfe. Their marriage brought peace to the colony for several years. In 1616, she visited England with her husband. There she was presented to the king, who treated her with great respect. However, on the return journey in 1617, she became ill and died. She was buried at Gravesend in England.

Pontiac's Rebellion

Native American uprising in 1763-1766. At the end of the **French and Indian War** (see p. 61), France surrendered its land in Canada to Great Britain. Britain then took control of forts, including Fort Detroit, around the Great Lakes. Pontiac, an

Pontiac's Vision

Pontiac's Rebellion (1763–1766) was not just an uprising against the English. Inspired by the teaching of Neolin, the Delaware Prophet, it was in part a religious revival, calling for return to the old Native American ways and rejection of European culture. Ottawa chief Pontiac, leader of the rebellion, recounted a vision of a visit to the Master of Life, or God. According to Pontiac, the Master of Life issued the following commands.

This land, where you live, I have made for you and not for others. How comes it that you suffer the whites on your lands? Can you not do without them? I know that those whom you call the children of your Great Father supply your wants, but if you were not bad, as you are, you would well do without them. You might live wholly as you did before you knew them. Before those whom you call your brothers came on your lands, did you not live by bow and arrow? You had no need of gun nor powder, nor the rest of their things, and nevertheless you caught animals to live and clothe yourselves with their skins, but when I saw that you inclined to the evil, I called back the animals into the depths of the woods, so that you had need of your brothers to have your wants supplied and cover you. You have only to become good and do what I want, and I shall send back to you the animals to live on. I do not forbid you, for all that, to suffer amongst you the children of your father. I love them, they know me and pray to me, and I give them their necessities and all that they bring to you, but as regards those who have come to trouble your country, drive them out, make war on them. I love them not, they know me not, they are my enemies and the enemies of your brothers. Send them back to the country which I made for them. There let them remain.

Source: Michigan Pioneer and Historical Collections.

Ottawa chief, had been allied with France. The British promised Pontiac that they would honor previous trade agreements and respect boundaries. Later, British General Jeffrey Amherst ended the French practice of giving gifts to Native Americans. These gifts included guns and firearms the Native Americans had begun to use for hunting. Pontiac formed a confederation of Ottawa, Huron, Potawatomi, and Seneca to stop the British from taking more land. By the end of 1763, his forces had taken 8 of 12 British forts.

At Fort Pitt, present-day Pittsburgh, under General Amherst's command, Captain Simeon Ecuyer sent the Native Americans "gifts" of blankets infected with smallpox. The result

Powhatan's Warning to John Smith

Powhatan, who was chief of the Powhatan Confederacy, came to know John Smith, leader of the English colony of Jamestown, Virginia. In 1609, disturbed by English mistreatment of his people, he gave Smith the following advice. After Powhatan's death in 1618, the advice was not followed, and the result was war with Powhatan's successor, Opechancanough (oh-puh-CAN-cuh-naw).

Why should you take by force that from us which you can have by love? Why should you destroy us, who have provided you with food? What can you get by war? We can hide our provisions, and fly into the woods; and then you must consequently famish by wronging your friends. What is the cause of your jealousy? You see us unarmed, and willing to supply your wants, if you will come in a friendly manner, and not with swords and guns, as to invade an enemy. I am not so simple, as not to know it is better to eat good meat, lie well, and sleep quietly with my women and children; to laugh and be merry with the English; and, being their friend, to have copper, hatchets, and whatever else I want, than to fly from all, to lie cold in the woods, feed upon acorns, roots, and such trash, and to be so hunted, that I cannot rest, eat, or sleep. In such circumstances, my men must watch, and if a twig should but break, all would cry out, "Here comes Capt. Smith"; and so, in this miserable manner, to end my miserable life; and, Capt. Smith, this might be soon your fate too, through your rashness and unadvisedness. I, therefore, exhort you to peaceable councils; and, above all, I insist that the guns and swords, the cause of all our jealousy and uneasiness, be removed and sent away.

Source: John Smith, *The Settlement at Jamestown.*

---

was an *epidemic* and many deaths among the Native Americans. Although Pontiac and his warriors had seized many British strongholds, they never took Fort Detroit or Fort Pitt. His efforts to enlist other nations in the rebellion were failing. Further, the supplies of weapons and ammunition he had hoped to obtain from the French never came. Finally, in 1766 Pontiac and other chiefs signed a treaty that forced them to open the Ohio Valley to British colonists.

Popé (*poh-PAY*)

Tewa (*TEE-wuh*) medicine man. Popé lived in the pueblo of San Juan on the Rio Grande. He rejected attempts by the Spanish to convert him and his people to Christianity. In 1680, Popé led the successful **Pueblo Revolt** (see p. 84), which drove the Spanish out of New Mexico for over 10 years. He was determined to destroy all Spanish influences. He punished anyone who did not practice Native American ways. Popé died in Santa Fe in 1688, four years before the Spanish retook the city.

Powhatan (*pow-HAT-un*)

Chief of the **Powhatan Confederacy** (see p. 44). The Powhatan nation occupied lands around the British settlement of Jamestown in Virginia. Their chief's name was Wahunsonacock. The settlers found this name too difficult and called him by the name of his nation of people, Powhatan. During the settlers' first winter in America (1607–1608), Powhatan provided them with food. The settlers began to steal his people's corn crop, and war broke out. Some colonists were taken prisoner. Powhatan's daughter, **Pocahontas** (see p. 79), is reputed to have saved the life of John Smith during this time. When settlers captured Pocahontas in 1613, Powhatan agreed to a peace treaty, which he kept to his death five years later.

Powhatan Wars

(See **Great Massacre**, p. 64)

Proclamation of 1763

British proclamation to limit westward expansion. At the end of the **French and Indian War** (see p. 61), Native Americans found many new British settlements on their lands. Ottawa chief Pontiac put together an alliance of nations to stop the new settlers. His rebellion was so successful that it alarmed the British. As a result, in 1763 King George III issued a proclamation. The Proclamation of 1763 banned British colonization west of the Appalachian Mountains. Settlers who were already west of the Appalachians were ordered to move back east. This was the first action taken by the British government that affected all **13 colonies** (see p. 87). The British thought the proclamation would protect colonial settlements and would reassure Native Americans. Some colonists saw it as interference in their right to live and trade where they chose. Others simply ignored it in their

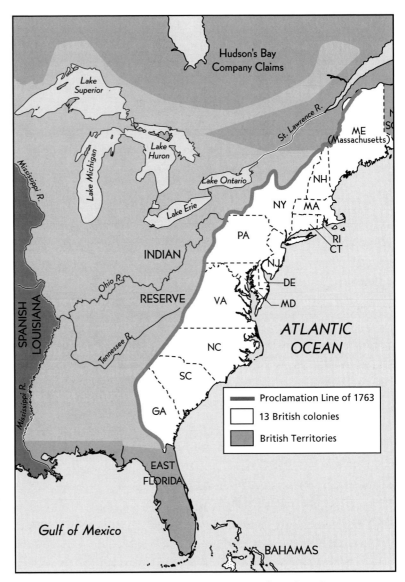

Following the end of the French and Indian War in 1763, Great Britain's government issued the Proclamation of 1763. The new law forbade American colonists to cross into lands west of the Appalachian Mountains. Those lands were to be set aside for Native Americans. Many colonists ignored the new law. The map above shows where the Proclamation Line was drawn.

search for good farmland. The proclamation remained in effect until 1776.

Pueblo Revolt

Native American rebellion in 1680 against Spanish in present-day New Mexico. The Spanish had conquered the Pueblo peoples of today's New Mexico. They then tried to force the native people to convert to Christianity. **Popé** (see p. 82), a Tewa medicine man, planned a revolt against the Spanish. The Tewa, Towa, Keres, **Hopi** (see p. 34), and Zuñi launched raids on Spanish settlements and farms. The success of these raids led to an attack on Santa Fe. Four hundred Spaniards were killed, and 2,500 settlers were driven out of the territory. The Spanish recaptured Santa Fe 12 years later. When they regained the territory, the Pueblo villages maintained their religious freedom.

Samoset

Abenaki (see p. 21) chief. Samoset (c.1590–c.1653) was the first Native American to approach the Pilgrims. He had learned some English from fishers near his home in present-day Maine. He greeted the Pilgrims by saying, "Welcome, Englishmen." He introduced the Pilgrims to **Squanto** (*SKWAN-toe*) (see p. 86), who also spoke English. Squanto helped prepare an agreement between the Pilgrims and the leader of the Wampanoag, Massasoit. In 1625, Samoset signed the first deed for the sale of Native American land to the English.

Spanish America

Spain's empire in North and South America, which lasted for more than 300 years. After **Columbus** (see p. 60) landed in the Bahamas, Spanish *conquistadors* (*cone-KEES-tuh-doors*), or conquerors, arrived in Central and South America. Their objectives were to explore and colonize, find gold, and enslave native peoples. When Hernán Cortés captured Mexico City, he destroyed the **Aztec** (see p. 24). This established Spain as the greatest power in the Americas. The Spanish later destroyed the **Inca** (see p. 34) Empire in South America. In North America, Spanish colonization spread into today's Southwest, up the Pacific coast to present-day California, and as far east as the Mississippi River and Florida.

The Spanish sent **missionaries** (see p. 70) throughout their American empire. The goal of the missions was to force Native Americans to convert to Catholicism. The missions also taught the Native Americans European agriculture and put them to work as laborers. Many Native Americans married Spanish colonists and established a new, mixed race called *mestizos* (*mes-TEEZ-ohs*). Native Americans sometimes rebelled against the

Spanish Atrocities

Spanish priest Bartolomé de Las Casas (1474–1566) was an outspoken champion of Native Americans. Having witnessed their mistreatment firsthand, he won passage of legislation that might have protected their rights had it ever been fully enforced. In his historical writings, Las Casas exposed Spanish atrocities, such as those on Hispaniola, described in this excerpt from his book *A Short Account of the Destruction of the Indies* (1542).

The Spaniards forced their way into native settlements, slaughtering everyone they found there, including small children, old men, pregnant women, and even women who had just given birth. . . . They even laid wagers on whether they could manage to slice a man in two at a stroke, or cut an individual's head from his body, or disembowel him with a single blow of their axes. They grabbed suckling infants by the feet and, ripping them from their mothers' breasts, dashed them headlong against the rocks. Others, laughing and joking all the while, threw them over their shoulders into a river, shouting, "Wriggle, you little perisher." . . . They spared no one, erecting especially wide gibbets on which they could string their victims up with their feet just off the ground and then burn them alive thirteen at a time, in honor of our Saviour and the twelve Apostles, or tie dry straw to their bodies and set fire to it.

Source: Bartolomé de Las Casas, *A Short Account of the Destruction of the Indies*

Spanish. The **Pueblo Revolt** (see p. 84) defeated the Spanish and drove them out of Santa Fe, New Mexico, for 12 years.

As Spain declined in power, it lost some American possessions. By the 1820s, most of Spain's American empire was lost in American colonial wars for independence. Puerto Rico and Cuba remained under Spanish rule until 1898. They were given up at the end of the Spanish-American War.

Squanto (*SKWAN-toe*)
Pawtuxet (*pah-TUX-it*) who came to aid Massachusetts Pilgrims. Squanto (c.1580–1622) was captured, enslaved, and brought to

Spain. He later spent time in England, where he learned to speak fluent English. When he returned to present-day Massachusetts in 1619, he joined the Wampanoag Nation. He served as an interpreter for **Massasoit** (see p. 69), the Wampanoag chief, in negotiating an agreement with the Plymouth Pilgrims. Squanto then lived among the Pilgrims, teaching them to plant crops. He also helped the Pilgrims in relations with other nations.

13 colonies

The British colonies in North America. There were three major European colonizers in the Americas: Great Britain, France, and Spain. Spain and France acquired large amounts of territory. Britain had less territory, but was the most successful at colonizing the land. Within a space of 125 years, the British established 13 colonies on the eastern border of the North American continent. The first settled was Virginia. It was created when settlers arrived at Jamestown in 1607. Other settlements led to the formation of more colonies: Massachusetts Bay, later named Massachusetts (1620), New York (1626), Maryland (1633), Rhode Island (1636), Connecticut (1636), Delaware (1638), New Hampshire (1638), North Carolina (1653), South Carolina (1663), New Jersey (1664), Pennsylvania (1682), and Georgia (1733).

Conflict arose almost immediately. The colonists claimed or purchased the land. The Native Americans did not understand the European concept of ownership. To American Indians, land could not be "owned." They believed it was a resource open to all for farming, hunting, and traveling. Ownership of the land was the reason most colonists had come to the New World. They viewed Native Americans as primitive peoples who did not use the land properly.

Events in Virginia set a pattern that was to be repeated throughout most of the colonies. When settlers arrived in Jamestown in 1607, the **Powhatan** (see p. 44) Nation provided food to get them through their first winter. The following year, the colonists expected an annual payment of corn. When John Smith and his men took it by force, the Powhatan retaliated. A truce was reached, but the settlers began claiming more land to grow tobacco. The Powhatan attacked, killing nearly a third of the colonists. The conflict continued until the Powhatan were forced out of Virginia or placed on small reservations.

Similarly, when the Pilgrims landed at Plymouth in 1620, the **Wampanoag** (see p. 48) greeted them with courtesy. On Chief **Massasoit**'s (see p. 69) orders, the settlers were shown how to plant corn and vegetables. In 1621, Massasoit agreed to a treaty that allowed thousands of colonists to arrive and settle peacefully. By 1661, they outnumbered the Wampanoag. Their growing demand for land finally led to **King Philip's War** (see p. 69) in 1675–1676. Other conflicts between Native Americans and colonists include the **Pequot War** (1636–1637) (see p. 78), which destroyed the **Pequot** (see p. 43) in Massachusetts and Connecticut; **Bacon's Rebellion** (1675–1676) (see p. 57), which saw attacks on the Nanticoke and Susquehannock in western Virginia; the **Tuscarora War** (1711–1713) (see p. 89), which drove the Tuscarora out of North Carolina; the 1765 raids in which *vigilantes* known as the **Paxton Boys** (see p. 77) massacred the Susquehannock in Pennsylvania (1763–1764); and **Lord Dunmore's War** (1774) (see p. 112), in which a **Shawnee**-led (see p. 45) confederacy of Native Americans failed to stop settlement of their lands in Virginia.

There were exceptions to the bleak picture of conflict between British colonists and Native Americans. Roger Williams, founder of Rhode Island, treated the Narragansett with respect. Pennsylvania founder **William Penn** (see p. 77) maintained peace with the **Delaware** (see p. 30) and Susquehannock. However, in most places, conflict was the rule. As the colonial population grew, many Native Americans migrated west beyond the Appalachian Mountains. They tried to escape war and the loss of their hunting and farming lands. By the mid-18th century, the colonists kept moving toward them, even over the Appalachians.

The British government tried to contain the growing conflict between Native Americans and colonists with treaties and the **Proclamation of 1763** (see p. 83). The proclamation banned colonization west of the Appalachians. Colonists ignored these measures and continued claiming ownership of Native American lands. Not surprisingly, when the American Revolution broke out in 1775, several Native American nations allied with the British.

Tuscarora War

A war between colonists and Native Americans in North Carolina lasting from 1711 to 1713. When settlers first arrived in that area, the Tuscarora Nation welcomed them. They aided them in battles against other Native Americans. Conflicts started when colonists began to settle on Tuscarora land. Traders cheated and enslaved them. A group of Swiss colonists established a settlement on Tuscarora land without making any payment. Tuscarora warriors began to raid outlying farms, killing 200 settlers. North Carolina called for help from South Carolina and Virginia. A colonial army led by Colonel James Moore attacked and defeated the Tuscarora. Four hundred warriors were taken prisoner and enslaved. The Tuscarora survivors escaped to the north. In 1722, they became the sixth nation in the **Iroquois Confederacy** (see p. 66).

West Indies

The chain of islands stretching from the southern tip of Florida to the northern part of South America. When **Christopher Columbus** (see p. 60) arrived in the West Indies, he thought he had reached the Far East. Europeans at that time referred to the Far Eastern countries of China and India as "the Indies." For this reason, he named the people who greeted him "Indians." In fact, they were the Arawak, who occupied much of the Bahamas and Hispaniola, which is today's Haiti and the Dominican Republic. The Arawak were farmers and fishers originally from South America.

Columbus established a small colony at Hispaniola in 1492 but found it destroyed when he returned the following year. The Spaniards he had left there had forced the **Arawak** (see p. 23) to look for gold rather than farm. Columbus reestablished the colony and began taking enslaved Arawak back to Spain. Using Hispaniola as a base, the Spanish established settlements on Puerto Rico, Cuba, and Jamaica over the next 30 years. Their interest, however, moved to the mainland after Hernán Cortés's expedition of 1519. They continued to use the Arawak for slave labor and raided other islands to capture more. The Arawak fought, but lost to their captors. They became virtually extinct from disease, hunger, slavery, and warfare. The Spanish then enslaved people from Africa to replace the Arawak laborers they had killed.

Columbus had discovered and named many of the Caribbean Islands. However, the first colonies there were not established until 1624, when the English founded a small settlement on the island of St. Kitts. The French arrived the same year, and both nations began extending their empires. They claimed individual islands up to the coast of South America. In 1630, the Dutch also seized some of the islands. The people of the Carib Nation who lived there offered only light resistance, although they managed to keep some of their land.

Over the next 200 years, control of the islands in the West Indies changed often. These changes followed the struggles for power in Europe. France and Holland kept some of their former colonies. However, many islands came under British rule due to the strength of Britain's Royal Navy. Some of the Carib peoples lived among their new rulers. Most were less harsh on the Native Americans than the Spaniards had been. European *diseases* inflicted severe losses on the Carib population.

CHAPTER THREE

The New Nation

The Young United States, 1764–1838

"[I have] fought for [my] countrymen, the squaws and papooses, against white men, who came, year after year, to cheat them and take away their lands. You know the cause of our making war. It is known to all white men. They ought to be ashamed of it."

—Black Hawk, Sac chief, after his defeat in the Black Hawk War, 1835

France lost an empire in the **French and Indian War** (see p. 61). In some ways, the Native Americans lost more. Gone were the respect and fair treatment they enjoyed as French allies. Gone was the chance to gain benefits from both France and Great Britain, such as trade goods or land security. The British colonists now viewed Native American nations that had allied with France as unfriendly. Those that had allied with Britain found their support did not stop settlers from moving onto their lands.

Many people in the **13 colonies** (see p. 87) were angered by the Proclamation of 1763. It banned colonization west of a boundary known as the Proclamation Line. This line ran from what is now Maine south through New York and Pennsylvania and along the Appalachian Mountains to Georgia (see map on p. 84). The settlers also believed it gave preferred treatment to Native Americans. Many chose to ignore the proclamation. For example, Virginia's governor, **Lord Dunmore** (see p. 112), granted land west of the Proclamation Line to veterans of the French and Indian War.

In 1774, the British passed the Quebec Act. It extended the Canadian border south to the Ohio River. It was another example of how Great Britain tried to keep colonial settlers out of the territory west of the Proclamation Line. Both the Proclamation of 1763 and the Quebec Act added to the decision by the 13 colonies to rebel. Their rebellion became known as the **American Revolution** (see p. 99). In 1776, the 13 colonies declared their independence as the United States of America.

The following year, the **Iroquois Confederacy** (see p. 66) split over what side to support in the American Revolution. The Cayuga, Mohawk, Onondaga, and Seneca joined the side of Great Britain. The Oneida and Tuscarora sided with the U.S. Further south, American forces at Fort Pitt attacked the **Shawnee** (see p. 45) and **Delaware** (see p. 30). The Shawnee and Delaware then joined with the **Cherokee** (see p. 25), **Choctaw** (see p. 27), **Chickasaw** (see p. 26), and **Creek** (see p. 29) nations on the side of the British.

When the Revolutionary War ended with the Treaty of Paris in 1783, the border of the U.S. was moved west. The U.S. now extended beyond the Appalachian Mountains to the Mississippi River. Boundary problems to the north and south did not stop the new nation's desire to expand. However, neither the Declaration of Independence nor the Treaty of Paris had considered Native Americans. Many Native nations in the eastern U.S. were punished for their support of the British. They had their lands taken away. In addition, settlers moving west were claiming new lands from the Native Americans living there. The patterns of the settlers on the east coast in the previous century were repeating themselves.

Timeline

1769

Spanish priest Junípero Serra founds a mission and presidio at San Diego, the start of a chain of missions built to convert Native Americans in California to Catholicism.

1775–1783

During the **American Revolution**, four nations of the Iroquois Confederacy—the Cayuga, Mohawk, Onondaga, and Seneca—side with the British. The Americans are aided by the other two nations, the Oneida and Tuscarora.

The Old Northwest refers to the territory that eventually became Ohio, Indiana, Illinois, Michigan, Wisconsin, and part of Minnesota. This region was home to many Native American nations. Some of these Native American nations had already been forced to move from the East. The new U.S. Congress issued the Ordinance of 1785. Under this ordinance, Native American acreage in the Northwest Territory would be sold to land companies. These companies, in turn, resold the acreage to settlers. The Treaty of Fort McIntosh also appeared in 1785. This treaty took land from the **Huron** (see p. 34), **Delaware** (see p. 30), **Ojibwa** (see p. 41), and Ottawa. In 1787, the federal government appeared to try and consider the Native Americans. It issued the Northwest Ordinance. This ordinance divided the Old Northwest into districts, which would later become states. It also stated that Indian "land and property shall never be taken away from them without their consent."

Settlers ignored these ordinances and **treaties** (see p. 122). They continued to move onto Native American lands. The Native Americans began attacks on the settlements that became known as the Wars for the Old Northwest. Among the wars and treaties of this time were **Little Turtle's War** (see p. 112), the Battle of Fallen Timbers, and the Treaty of Greenville (Ohio). In all the wars, the Native Americans were eventually defeated. Under the treaties they lost most of their land.

For the Delaware, the signing of the Treaty of Greenville marked the end of a long period of fighting for their land. One historian noted that the

1781	1787	1789	1790–1795
The Yuma Uprising takes place against Spanish rule in southwestern Arizona and southeastern California.	Delegates from all 13 states meet in Philadelphia to begin writing the U.S. Constitution. The same year, the Northwest Ordinance provides for development of the Old Northwest into states while, in word only, affirming Native American rights.	George Washington becomes the first president of the United States.	**Little Turtle's War**, named for Miami leader Little Turtle, rages in the Ohio River valley. The U.S. wins a decisive victory in the Battle of Fallen Timbers (1794). Native Americans give up Ohio and part of Indiana in the Treaty of Greenville (1795).

Delaware went through a forty years' war. First they fought against Great Britain, and later the U.S. The Delaware conflicts began in 1755, during the French and Indian War. They continued until the Treaty of Greenville in 1795. For other Native Americans, the wars went on.

U.S. expansion and Native American loss of land continued with the Louisiana Purchase of 1803. **Thomas Jefferson** (see p. 109) had foreseen a U.S. that extended from coast to coast. The U.S. bought the Louisiana Territory from France. This was the vast area between the Mississippi River and the Rocky Mountains. Jefferson sent Meriwether Lewis and William Clark on their famous expedition (see **Lewis and Clark expedition**, p. 110). Their goals were to explore the territory and to look for a water route to the Pacific Coast. Jefferson thought he could persuade Native Americans to become farmers and foresters. He also thought the native nations would eventually adapt to the European cultures of the U.S. settlers. Jefferson saw the Louisiana Territory as a large reservation for all Native Americans, with European Americans settled on the lands east of the Mississippi. What he did not foresee was that settlers would claim Native American land across the continent in less than five generations.

One of the Native American leaders who had refused to sign the Treaty of Greenville was Tecumseh (see **Tecumseh's Rebellion**, p. 118). He was a **Shawnee** (see p. 45) and one of the most important of all Native American leaders. He understood that Native Americans had to unite from the Gulf of

1802	1803	1809–1813	1809–1821
The **Tlingit** destroy the Russian settlement of New Archangel (Sitka), Alaska.	The United States buys the Louisiana Territory from France. This brings many more Native American nations into U.S. territory. The next year, **Lewis and Clark** begin to explore the Louisiana Territory and the Northwest for a passage to the Pacific coast.	In **Tecumseh's Rebellion**, Shawnee chief Tecumseh tries to unite the Native American nations but is defeated.	**Sequoyah** creates the Cherokee syllabary (characters that represent syllables instead of letters), giving the Cherokee a written language.

Mexico to Canada. In 1809, he began traveling the Mississippi. He was trying to persuade Native American nations to act together. While Tecumseh was away, **William Henry Harrison** (see p. 103) tricked Tecumseh's brother **Tenskwatawa** (see p. 118) into attacking Harrison's forces. The attack resulted in the **Battle of Tippecanoe** (see p. 120). The outcome of the battle discouraged many nations from joining **Tecumseh's Rebellion** (see p. 118).

The **War of 1812** (see p. 123) saw many Native American nations siding with the British. They did this once again, in hopes of stopping further U.S. settlement. Again, a series of wars and treaties between the Native Americans and the U.S. occurred. Again, there was defeat and loss of lands for the native nations. Among these wars were the **Creek War** (see p. 102), the First **Seminole War** (see p. 117), and the Treaty of Horseshoe Bend.

During the years that followed the War of 1812, many of the Native Americans living north of the Ohio River were pushed westward off their lands for good. Some nations, such as the Kickapoo (see **Kickapoo Resistance**, p. 110), put up a strong fight, and many would remain in the area until the 1860s.

Spain was gradually losing power in North America. In 1819, Spain sold Florida to the U.S. In the Pacific Northwest, Russia claimed Alaska. This threatened Spain's claim to the continent's west coast. In an effort to maintain its claim, Spain founded a chain of missions in California. The first mission was in San Diego in 1769. The chain reached San Francisco by 1776. Spain's treatment of native peoples in California was similar to that

1811	**1812–1814**	**1815–1825**	**1817–1818**
Fur merchant John Jacob Astor founds Astoria, Oregon, a center for trading with Native Americans in the Pacific Northwest.	During the **War of 1812**, Tecumseh fights for the British against the U.S. By 1814, the **Creek War** ends.	Treaties signed north of the Ohio River begin the westward removal of that region's Native Americans.	In the First **Seminole War**, the Seminole in Florida (then owned by Spain) clash with the U.S. over the Seminole's harboring of fugitive slaves.

elsewhere in Spanish America. Native Americans were forced to convert to Catholicism, enslaved, and required to learn European trades and farming practices. Many resisted, and there were numerous uprisings. One of the best-known was the Yuma Uprising in 1781, which took place along the border between California and Arizona.

In Alaska, the Russians also faced Native American uprisings. In 1803, **Tlinglit** (see p. 47) warriors destroyed the Russian settlement of New Archangel, Alaska. Meanwhile, as the 19th century began, Russian, British, and American fur trappers and traders often visited the Pacific Northwest. Among them were men such as William Ashley and Andrew Henry, who developed a system for supplying trappers and traders in the Rocky Mountains with food, tools, and other equipment. Another important figure was John Jacob Astor, an American who founded Astoria, Oregon, which became a center of trade between American fur trappers and local Native Americans. Along with European goods, the traders also brought European diseases such as cholera, smallpox, and influenza that devastated the Native American nations.

In 1821, Mexico won independence from Spain. Native Americans of California and the Southwest were now members of the new Mexican nation. East of the Mississippi, Native American uprisings continued against U.S. settlers. These included the **Winnebago Uprising** (see p. 126) and the **Black Hawk War** (see p. 101). The Sac chief, Black Hawk, was defeated at Bad Axe River in Wisconsin. This was the last battle in the Wars for the Old

1819–1833	1819	1823–1825	1830
In the **Kickapoo Resistance**, the Kickapoo fight their removal from the Illinois Country.	The United States acquires Florida from Spain, putting the Seminole under official U.S. jurisdiction.	William H. Ashley and Andrew Henry develop the brigade-rendezvous system for financing and supplying fur trappers and traders in the Rocky Mountains. Skirmishes between these mountain men and local Native Americans become common.	The Indian Removal Act is passed, requiring the relocation of eastern nations to the west.

Northwest. Following Black Hawk's defeat, the Sac and Fox nations were led by **Keokuk** (see p. 109), who had opposed Black Hawk's fight.

Some Native Americans tried peaceful ways of dealing with the U.S. The Choctaw, Chickasaw, Cherokee, Creek, and Seminole of the Southeast were sometimes called the "**Five Civilized Tribes**" (see p. 103) because of their willingness to adopt white ways to get along with white settlers. **Sequoyah** (see p. 117), a Cherokee, even created a new alphabet so that his people could communicate with a written language.

In some cases, Native Americans tried to use U.S. laws to protect themselves and their land. These cases had to do with defining the relationship between Native American nations, the U.S., and individual states. In the 1831 case of *Cherokee Nation* v. *State of Georgia*, the Cherokee asked the U.S. Supreme Court to stop Georgia from making Cherokee people obey Georgia's laws. However, the court decided that it had no right to rule on a case brought by a Native American nation against a U.S. state.

The next year, the Supreme Court did take a case involving the Cherokee. *Worcester* v. *State of Georgia* was brought on behalf of a white man named Samuel Worcester who had been living with the Cherokee. In the case, the Cherokee again argued that they should not be subject to Georgia laws. This time the court ruled in their favor.

The Supreme Court's decision in *Worcester* v. *State of Georgia* victory was ignored. President **Andrew Jackson** (see p. 108) refused to enforce the Supreme

1830–1833	1831	1831–1834	1832
As the European presence grows on the west coast, influenza and other diseases sweep through Native American communities in California, Oregon, and British Columbia.	In *Cherokee Nation* v. *State of Georgia,* the Supreme Court refuses to rule on whether Cherokee are subject to state laws.	The Choctaw are forced to move to Indian Territory.	In *Worcester* v. *State of Georgia*, the Supreme Court declares Georgia's Indian laws unconstitutional, a temporary victory for the Cherokee. The same year, the Sac and Fox resist removal from Illinois, but are defeated in the **Black Hawk War**.

Court decision. In 1830, he had signed the Indian Removal Act. This act called for the relocation of eastern Native American nations and included those in the Old Northwest and the Southeast. The Native American nations were to be moved to the newly created **Indian Territory** (see p. 106) west of the Mississippi. Thousands of Native Americans died from hunger, disease, and exposure on their forced westward migrations. The Choctaw were the first to move west, beginning in 1831.

In 1832, Congress approved the creation of the **Bureau of Indian Affairs** (see p. 104) to protect Native Americans. Still, their rights were ignored. In a few more years, other nations, such as the Chickasaw and Creek, were forced west as well. In 1835, after **Elias Boudinot** (see p. 101), **John Ridge** (see p. 115), and 18 other Cherokee leaders signed the Treaty of New Echota, the Cherokee also moved west. Their eviction from their homelands became known as the **Trail of Tears** (see p. 121). Some Seminole fought off removal during the Second **Seminole War** (see p. 117). (The First Seminole War took place in 1817–1818.) But by the time of the Trail of Tears, most eastern nations had been forced west of the Mississippi River. Life in the West would be no easier for the Native Americans. They would continue to be forced off their lands in the years ahead.

1834	1835–1842	1837	1838–1839
Congress creates the **Bureau of Indian Affairs**.	In the Second Seminole War, the Seminole, led by **Chief Osceola**, fight against the U.S. (A Third Seminole War is fought in 1855–1858.)	The removal of the Chickasaw begins. The same year, a smallpox epidemic ravages the Mandan, Hidatsa, and Arikara nations along the upper Missouri River. Through 1870, at least four smallpox epidemics will attack Native Americans in the West.	Forced to leave Georgia following the Treaty of New Echota (1835), the Cherokee migrate to Oklahoma on the **Trail of Tears**. More than 4,000 of the 15,000 Cherokee involved die on the journey.

A-Z of Key People, Events, and Terms

American Revolution

The American colonies' war for independence from Great Britain, lasting from 1775 to 1783. The British **Proclamation of 1763** (see p. 83 and map on p. 84) was among the many causes of the American Revolution. The proclamation banned settlers from moving west of the Appalachian Mountains. This was the territory that was reserved for Native Americans. Colonists thought the proclamation interfered in their right to seek new land. Many ignored it and continued to move west onto Native American lands. As a result, when the American Revolution began, many Native American nations sided with the British.

The powerful **Iroquois Confederacy** (see p. 66) split when the chiefs took different sides. The Mohawk, Seneca, and Cayuga battled with the British against the American colonists. The Oneida and Tuscarora supported the Americans. The Onondaga tried to remain neutral, but finally joined the British.

The split in the confederacy began a civil war among the previously allied native nations. The Mohawk destroyed Oneida villages. At the Battle of Oriskany (*oh-RIS-kuh-nee*), New York, Mohawk and Seneca on the British side fought Oneida and Tuscarora on the American side. In Pennsylvania, a Seneca and Cayuga force attacked and destroyed several American settlements. When American forces won the Battle of Newtown, the British and their Native American allies stopped the attacks in the area.

The region located near Lake Erie was called the Old Northwest. Many battles took place in this area. American forces there attacked the Shawnee and Delaware. The **Huron** (see p. 34) and Shawnee attacked American settlements in Kentucky. In 1781, the **Chickasaw** (see p. 26) joined the British in taking Fort Jefferson.

In the South, Cherokee raids began against American settlements. The Chickamauga (*chik-uh-MAWG-uh*) conducted raids

The Second Treaty of Fort Stanwix

Four of six Iroquois nations— the Cayuga, Mohawk, Onondaga, and Seneca—sided with Britain during the American Revolution. After the war, peace with the United States was made in New York with the Second Treaty of Fort Stanwix (1784). (The First Treaty of Fort Stanwix had been signed between Britain and the Iroquois before the war, in 1768.) The other two Iroquois nations, the Oneida and Tuscarora, who had supported the U.S. in the war, were also involved. The treaty, excerpted below, weakened the Iroquois Confederacy by forbidding individual nations from negotiating on behalf of any others.

The United States of America give peace to the Senecas, Mohawks, Onondagas, and Cayugas, and receive them into their protection upon the following conditions:

Article I.
Six hostages shall be immediately delivered to the commissioners by the said nations, to remain in possession of the United States, till all the prisoners, white and black, which were taken . . . in the late war, from among the people of the United States, shall be delivered up.

Article II.
The Oneida and Tuscarora nations shall be secured in the possession of the lands on which they are settled.

Article III.
A line shall be drawn, beginning at the mouth of a creek about four miles east of Niagara...the said line from the mouth of the [creek] to the Ohio River shall be the western boundary of the lands of the Six Nations, so that the Six Nations shall and do yield to the United States, all claims to the country west of the said boundary, and then they shall be secured in the peaceful possession of the lands they inhabit east and north of the same, reserving only six miles square round the fort of Oswego, to the United States, for the support of the same.

Source: National Archives.

against colonists in the Tennessee Valley. The Chickasaw raided settlements as far north as Kentucky. The **Choctaw** (see p. 27) and **Creek** (see p. 29) fought for the British along the lower Mississippi River and in Georgia and Tennessee.

In 1783, British and American representatives signed a treaty ending the war known as the Treaty of Paris because it was signed in Paris, France. As part of the agreement, the Mississippi became the western boundary of the new U.S. Americans now claimed land in what had been Native American territory. The Oneida and Tuscarora received extra lands for their support of the Americans. However, these grants of land were later lost to further American settlement.

Black Hawk War

The last Native American struggle for the Old Northwest. In 1804, the Sac and Fox nations lived in what is now Illinois. They signed a treaty and agreed to move west of the Mississippi River. Many of the people did not believe in the treaty and resisted being moved. The Sac chief Black Hawk led these people. By 1830, nearly all the Sac and Fox had been moved into today's Iowa. Black Hawk and his followers repeatedly tried to return to their Illinois village. In 1832, he arrived there with 400 warriors and their families to grow corn. Allies from other Native American nations joined him. They were met with a force of soldiers and agreed to return to Iowa. The truce failed and Black Hawk attacked American troops in a battle called Stillman's Run.

Black Hawk's army retreated north to Wisconsin. The American troops followed them. Black Hawk was defeated in a battle at the Bad Axe River. He escaped, but later surrendered. After Black Hawk's surrender, the Sac pledged never to live, hunt, or fish in their Illinois homeland.

Boudinot, Elias

Cherokee (see p. 25) writer and editor. Boudinot (1803–1839) published a book called *Poor Sarah*. This book was about the conversion of a Native American girl to Christianity. It may be the first work of Native American fiction. Boudinot was the first editor of the first Indian newspaper, called the *Cherokee Phoenix*. The paper used **Sequoyah**'s (see p. 117) Cherokee alphabet. Boudinot was murdered for his support of Cherokee removal to the west.

Brant, Joseph

Mohawk chief. Brant was born in the Ohio Valley in 1742 and named Thayendanegea *(thay-en-dan-uh-GAY-uh)*. He grew up in New York as a friend of British colonial official **Sir William**

Joseph Brant.
(Library of Congress)

Johnson (see p. 67). He fought with Johnson in the **French and Indian War** (see p. 61). Brant was an educated man who knew English as well as several Native American languages. During the **American Revolution** (see p. 99), Brant helped convince four of the six nations of the **Iroquois Confederacy** (see p. 66) to side with Great Britain against the colonists. He led Iroquois forces at the Battle of Oriskany and many raids on frontier settlements. After the war, the British rewarded Brant and his followers with tracts of land in Canada. There, Brant continued to advise the British in their relations with Native Americans.

Clark, George Rogers

Soldier. Clark (1752–1818) was a surveyor who was born in Virginia. He became involved in **Lord Dunmore's War** (see p. 112), which was a conflict with Shawnee and Ottawa Indians. Clark became a hero of the **American Revolution** (see p. 99). He began his war experiences by commanding forces in Kentucky against Native Americans. As a general, he battled against Native American nations throughout the Old Northwest. There he became known as an "Indian fighter." After the war, Clark headed a land-grant commission. He also consulted on Indian affairs in the Ohio Valley.

Cornplanter

Seneca leader at Battle of Fort Stanwix. Cornplanter (1740–1836) was the son of a Seneca woman and a European man. The **American Revolution** (see p. 99) brought about a split in the Iroquois Confederacy. The Seneca joined the Mohawk, Onondaga, and Cayuga in fighting alongside the British. In 1777, Iroquois warriors joined British forces in an attack on the American Fort Stanwix. Seneca chiefs Cornplanter and Old Smoke and Mohawk chief **Joseph Brant** (see p. 101) led the attack. Cornplanter continued to lead war parties against the Americans. In 1784 he signed the Treaty of Fort Stanwix. Later he worked for Seneca rights and tribal lands in western New York State.

Cornplanter.
(Library of Congress)

Creek War

War between **Creek** (see p. 29) and American forces fought from 1813 to 1814. The Creek peoples lived in what are now

Georgia and Alabama. Early English settlers gave them their name because they built their villages along rivers and creeks. The Creek divided each of their villages into "red towns" and "white towns." Warriors called Red Sticks lived in the red towns. They raided for honor or revenge. Peacemakers called White Sticks lived in the white towns. During **Tecumseh's Rebellion** (see p. 118), Tecumseh traveled south seeking support. Many Creek joined him in fighting the U.S.

In 1813, a force of Red Sticks attacked Fort Mims, near Mobile on the Alabama River. Federal and state troops eventually defeated the Red Sticks. After their defeat, both the Red Sticks and White Sticks were forced to sign the Treaty of Horseshoe Bend. Under this treaty, the Creek lost 23 million acres of land. Baton Rouge, the capital of Louisiana, means Red Sticks in French.

Five Civilized Tribes

Term for five nations in the Southeast **culture area** (see p. 30): the **Choctaw** (see p. 27), **Chickasaw** (see p. 26), **Cherokee** (see p. 25), **Creek** (see p. 29), and **Seminole** (see p. 116). The name arose because these nations behaved in ways that European Americans considered civilized. They farmed, lived in permanent homes, wore European-style clothes, and had organized governments. The Cherokee also had their own form of writing and their own newspaper. Despite being "civilized," the Five Civilized Tribes were forced to move west as a result of Indian removal policy.

Harrison, William Henry

Soldier; ninth U.S. president. Born in 1773, Harrison began his military career in 1791. Later, he took part in General **Anthony Wayne**'s (see p. 124) battles against a *confederation* of **Shawnee** (see p. 45), **Miami** (see p. 38), and **Ojibwa** (see p. 41) in what is now Indiana. These actions ended in the Battle of Fallen Timbers and the Treaty of Greenville. As U.S. secretary of the Northwest Territory, he violated the treaty. Harrison wrote laws to open up the area to settlers. Next, in his career as governor of Indiana Territory, he persuaded the Sac and Fox nations to sign away lands in today's Illinois. He again violated

William Henry Harrison. (Library of Congress)

the treaty and took 2.5 million acres of Native American land under the Treaty of Fort Wayne.

In 1811 Harrison's forces defeated Native Americans at the **Battle of Tippecanoe** (see p. 120) and the Battle of the Thames. Years later, he used his reputation as an Indian fighter when he ran for president in 1840. He used the slogan "Tippecanoe and Tyler too." Harrison won the election but died after only a month in office.

Spending by the Indian Department

In the first half of the 19th century, the federal government dealt with Native Americans through various superintendents of Indian affairs, and, from 1824, through a central Bureau of Indian Affairs. All such institutions came broadly under the heading of the Indian Department or Indian Service. Whatever it was called, the annual costs of the Indian Department went up by more than 60 times from 1791 to 1833. The increased spending included annual payments and other compensation for land purchases from Native American tribes; the costs of relocating tribes; and educational services.

Years	Total Expenditures
1791–1800	$311,339
1801–1810	$802,338
1811–1820	$1,731,116
1821–1830	$5,280,354

Source: U.S. Department of the Interior.

Indian Affairs, Bureau of

In 1824, the Bureau of Indian Affairs (BIA) was created. It was part of the War Department and replaced the old Office of Indian Trade. In 1832, Congress formally approved the BIA. The president was in charge of appointing a commissioner for Indian affairs. In 1849, the BIA was moved to the new Department of the Interior. This happened at a time when most Native nations were suffering from disease and starvation. The condition of the Native Americans was a result of their removal to reservations. This meant the new BIA had to provide food and other supplies.

The BIA was formed to protect Native Americans. However, it did not stop states from passing laws that took away Native American lands and legal rights. The Meriam Report of 1938 listed the problems with the system. In the 1970s a new policy was put in place. Native American cultures and tribal governments were accepted. The BIA is now a group that advises on Native American affairs.

Indian removal policy

A plan to move Native American nations to a different area. This policy began when the first settlers arrived on the east coast and took Native American land. It became a formal policy at the beginning of the 19th century. **Thomas Jefferson** (see p. 109) believed Native Americans should become "civilized." He thought they should farm the lands west of the Mississippi River. Settlers along the east coast wanted more land. **Andrew Jackson** (see p. 108) persuaded **Cherokee** (see p. 25) leaders to give up their lands in Georgia and move to Arkansas Territory. Native Americans were often divided about whether to agree to give up land and move elsewhere.

From 1817 to 1818, the U.S. fought the **Seminole** (see p. 116) Nation in the First Seminole War. The Seminole had been allowing runaway enslaved Africans to live among them for protection. The war convinced Jackson that Native Americans had to be moved out of the East. As president, he signed the Indian Removal Act. This Act would cause eastern Native American nations to move to the Indian Territory west of the Mississippi.

Individual states were also putting pressure on Native American nations to move west. In Georgia, the Cherokee argued before the Supreme Court. Their case was called *Cherokee Nation* v. *State of Georgia*. The Cherokee told the court that they and other Native American peoples were independent nations. The court ruled that they were not independent nations. Instead, the court called them "domestic dependent nations." In this term, the court meant that the Native Americans had a relation to the United States like that of "a *ward* to his guardian." The court also said that it could not rule on a case between a Native American nation and U.S. state. In the case called *Worcester* v. *State of Georgia*, the Supreme Court said that only the federal

Native Americans Removed West of the Mississippi River by the United States, 1831–1838

From 1831 to 1838, the number of eastern Native Americans relocated west of the Mississippi River increased sharply, as the following table shows.

Year	Number
1831	5,407
1832	5,500
1833	5,462
1834	4,386
1835	2,330
1836	15,948
1837	9,688
1838	25,139
Total	73,860

government could direct Indian affairs. This meant that states such as Georgia could not decide what would happen to the Native Americans. This ruling was ignored, and the Cherokee were removed from Georgia. The Cherokee were forced to move to **Indian Territory** (see below) on the **Trail of Tears** (1838–1839) (see p. 121).

The Cherokee were not the only nation to be removed. Thousands of Native Americans would be forced to leave their homelands in the southeast U.S. during the 1830s. The first were the Choctaw, who had helped Jackson win the Battle of New Orleans. They were moved to Oklahoma in 1831. Of the 13,000 who migrated, 4,000 died of exposure, hunger, or *disease*. Under the Indian Removal Act, the Creek were moved from Alabama and Georgia in 1836; the Chickasaw from Mississippi in 1837–1838; and the Cherokee in 1838–1839. Some of the **Seminole** (see p. 116) from Florida were moved. Many retreated into the swamplands. When the Seminole Wars ended in 1858, they agree to be relocated. However, the Seminole Nation never signed a treaty, and many Seminole stayed in Florida.

The Indian Removal Act was not used again after 1839. Later, the forced relocations of nations onto reservations were agreed to by treaty. Jackson had made it clear that the wishes of the federal government came before the rights of Native Americans. The United States kept the right to decide where American Indians should live throughout the 19th century.

Indian Territory

Lands put aside for Native Americans west of the Mississippi. The term "Indian Territory" came into use in the 1820s. President James Monroe suggested that Native Americans be given their own land west of the Mississippi River. The "Indian Territory" became the area that stretched north from Texas to today's Nebraska. Most people thought this was a good idea. Those who fought for the Native Americans' rights saw the territory as a permanent home for them. Those who disliked native peoples saw it as a way of confining them to one place.

Many nations already lived in the northern parts of the territory. The region to the south became the home of those Native American nations who were forced to migrate under President

Andrew Jackson on Indian Removal

In his annual message to Congress on December 6, 1830, President Andrew Jackson spelled out the reasons why the provisions of the Indian Removal Act, passed earlier that year, should be promptly carried out. The act called for the relocation of eastern Native American nations to new lands west of the Mississippi. According to Jackson, that policy was good for the country, the states, and the Indians themselves.

The consequence of a speedy removal will be important to the United States, to individual states, and to the Indians themselves. The [financial] advantages which it promises to the government are the least of its recommendations. It puts an end to all possible danger of collision between the authorities of the general and state governments on account of the Indians. It will place a dense and civilized population in large tracts of country now occupied by a few savage hunters. By opening the whole territory between Tennessee on the north and Louisiana on the south to the settlement of the whites it will [greatly] strengthen the southwestern frontier and render the adjacent states strong enough to repel future invasions without remote aid. It will relieve the whole state of Mississippi and the western part of Alabama of Indian occupancy, and enable those states to advance rapidly in population, wealth, and power. It will separate the Indians from immediate contact with settlements of whites; free them from the power of the states; enable them to pursue happiness in their own way and under their own rude institutions; will retard the progress of decay, which is lessening their numbers; and perhaps cause them gradually, under the protection of the government and through the influence of good counsels, to cast off their savage habits and become an interesting, civilized, and Christian community. These consequences, some of them so certain and the rest so probable, make the complete execution of the plan sanctioned by Congress at their last session [the 1830 Indian Removal Act] an object of much solicitude.

Source: National Archives.

Andrew Jackson's (see p. 108) Indian removal policy (see p. 104). The territory had no formal government or exact borders. Over time, nations in the north were persuaded or forced to sell much of their land. The entire area was also being used by a growing number of settlers. The Indian Territory was reduced in size until it became today's Oklahoma.

A Choctaw Farewell

In 1831, the Choctaw in Mississippi became the first Native American nation to move west under the Indian Removal Act (1830). They went reluctantly, in compliance with the Treaty of Dancing Rabbit Creek (1830), which had been marred by bribery of tribal representatives. In 1832, tribal leader George W. Harkins spoke about the Choctaw "expulsion" in a "Farewell Letter to the American People."

It is said that our present movements are our own voluntary acts—such is not the case. We found ourselves like a benighted stranger, following false guides, until he was surrounded on every side, with fire or water. The fire was certain destruction, and feeble hope was left him of escaping by water. A distant view of the opposite shore encourages the hope; to remain would be utter annihilation. Who would hesitate, or would say that his plunging into the water was his own voluntary act? Painful in the extreme is the mandate of our expulsion. We regret that it should proceed from the mouth of our professed friend, and for whom our blood was commingled with that of his bravest warriors, on the field of danger and death.

But such is the instability of professions. The man who said that he would plant a stake and draw a line around us, that never should be passed, was the first to say he could not guard the lines, and drew up the stake and wiped out all traces of the line. I will not conceal from you my fears, that the present grounds may be removed—I have my foreboding—who of us can tell after witnessing what has already been done, what the next force may be.

I ask you in the name of justice, for repose for myself and my injured people. Let us alone—we will not harm you, we want rest.

Source: George Harkins, "Farewell Letter to the American People."

Jackson, Andrew

General; seventh U.S. president. Before joining the army, Jackson (1767–1845) was a lawyer, congressman, senator, judge, and planter. He was the commander of the Tennessee *militia* and he defeated the Creek (see p. 29) in the Creek War (1813–1814) (see p. 102). The Creek were forced to give up 23 million acres of land. Jackson also won, with the aid of the Choctaw (see p. 27), the Battle of New Orleans.

Jackson believed in expanding U.S. territory. He forced a treaty on the Cherokee (see p. 25) in Georgia, making them emigrate to today's Oklahoma. In 1817, at the request of Georgia planters who wanted more land, he led raids into **Seminole** (see p. 116) territory in Florida. This started the First Seminole War. Elected president in 1828, he served two terms (1829–1837). In 1830, he signed the Indian Removal Act. This law required all Native Americans in the South to move west of the Mississippi River. Two years later, the Supreme Court ruled in favor of the Cherokee in their suit against the state of Georgia. However, Jackson ignored the ruling and continued to support Indian removal.

Jefferson, Thomas

Third U.S. president; statesman. Prior to his two terms as president (1801–1809), Jefferson (1743–1826) wrote the Declaration of Independence (1776). He served as governor of Virginia, U.S. minister to France, secretary of state, and vice president. A highlight of his presidency was the Louisiana Purchase (1803). This land purchase more than doubled the size of the U.S. It also placed thousands of Native Americans under U.S. law. Jefferson wanted to move all eastern native peoples into the country's new territory. Here they would learn European ways and become farmers. To accomplish this, he asked territorial governors to acquire land and remove the Native Americans. He thought it would take 50 generations for Europeans to settle the lands west of the Mississippi River. However, the settlers actually displaced Native Americans across the continent less than 100 years after the Louisiana Purchase.

Keokuk.
(Library of Congress)

Keokuk (*KEE-oh-cook*)

Sac Chief (1780–1848). In 1804, leaders of the Sac and Fox nations gave up their lands in today's Illinois. During this time, Keokuk became a Sac chief. He wanted to make peace with the Americans. His plan was opposed by another Sac named Black Hawk (see **Black Hawk War**, p. 101). Keokuk and other Native American leaders went to Washington to bargain for peace with the U.S. government. Keokuk became chief of the combined Sac and Fox nations. He signed another treaty in which more Native American lands were given up. The Sac lived peacefully in Iowa until 1842. At that time, settlers forced Keokuk to sell all but 40 acres of Sac land in Iowa.

Kickapoo Resistance

Native American conflict (1819–1833). The Kickapoo lived in the Illinois country. This area was in present-day Illinois and Indiana. In 1819, the federal government relocated some Kickapoo to the west. Two bands of Kickapoo decided to stay and resist. Mecina led one group. They fought a war against the settlers. Federal and state military action stopped the war. Mecina then joined the other band, led by Kennekuk. Kennekuk did not fight. He stalled by promising to move westward. He would then offer excuses for delay. In 1832, many of his followers joined Sac and Fox leader Black Hawk in the **Black Hawk War** (see p. 101). After the war, Kennekuk's band finally moved to Kansas.

Lewis and Clark expedition

An exploration of North America that took place between 1804 and 1806. **Thomas Jefferson** (see p. 109) became president in 1801. He had long wanted to see if there was a river passage to

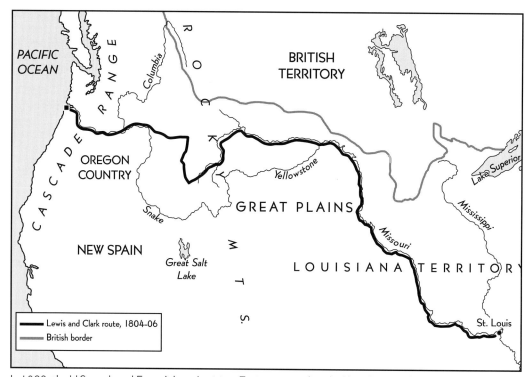

In 1803, the U.S. purchased France's huge Louisiana Territory, more than doubling the size of the U.S. The next year, President Thomas Jefferson sent Meriwether Lewis and William Clark to explore the new lands.

A Memory of Lewis and Clark

From 1832 to 1836, painter George Catlin (1796–1872) lived in the West, painting portraits and scenes of Native American life beyond the U.S. frontier. He wanted to preserve a record of traditional American Indian ways before they were gone. In some cases, Catlin's paintings and notes are our only record of nations that shortly thereafter became extinct. Yet he was not the first to penetrate the West in this era of exploration. In North Dakota, he came across a Hidatsa (huh-DAT-suh) chief who remembered getting a visit from explorers Meriwether Lewis and William Clark 30 years earlier.

The chief . . . of this tribe is a very ancient man by the name of Eeh-tohk-pah-shee-pee-shah (The Black Moccasin). He counts more than an hundred snows. For some days I have been an inmate in his hospitable lodge. He sits tottering with age, and silently reigns sole monarch of the little community around him. They continually drop in to cheer his sinking energies and to render him their homage. His voice and sight are nearly gone, but the gestures of his hand are still energetic and youthful, and speak the language of his heart.

I have been treated in the kindest manner by this old chief. I have painted his portrait as he was seated on the floor of his lodge smoking his pipe, and he recounting to me some of the extraordinary feats of his life. He sits with a beautiful Crow robe wrapped around him, his hair wound up in a conical form upon his head, and fastened with a small wooden pin to keep it in its place.

He has many distinct recollections of Lewis and Clark, the first explorers of this country, who crossed the Rocky Mountains thirty years ago. They too were treated with great kindness by Black Moccasin. In consequence, they constituted him chief of the tribe, with the consent of his people. He has remained their chief ever since. He enquired very earnestly for "Red Hair" and "Long Knife."

I told him that "Long Knife" [Lewis] has been dead many years but "Red Hair" [Clark] was still living in St. Louis, and would be glad to hear of him. He seemed much pleased, and has signified to me that he will make me bearer of some particular dispatches to him.

Source: George Catlin, *Letters and Notes on the North American Indians.*

the Pacific Ocean. He decided to send a military expedition across the continent. Jefferson chose Meriwether Lewis to lead it. Lewis and his co-captain, William Clark, had several goals. They wanted to learn all they could about the Native Americans they would meet. They were also to tell the native nations about the

Louisiana Purchase. Lewis and Clark would explain to the Native Americans that their nations were now part of the U.S.

The Lewis and Clark expedition left St. Louis in 1804. It followed the Missouri River to the Rocky Mountains and then the Columbia River to the Pacific. They met and studied many Native American nations along the way. These included the **Sioux** (see p. 46), **Mandan** (see p. 37), **Hidatsa** (see p. 34), **Shoshone** (see p. 45), and **Nez Percé** (see p. 41), among others. While visiting the Mandan, Lewis and Clark met a young Shoshone woman named **Sacajawea** (*sack-uh-juh-WAY-uh*) (see p. 116). For the rest of the journey, she served as their translator.

As the group moved west, formal councils were held to convince the nations to stop trading with the British and deal only with Americans. Lewis and Clark also tried to offer peace agreements among warring nations. Their studies of the Native Americans of that time have proved helpful to historians today.

Little Turtle's War

Native lands in the Ohio River valley had been lost when the British were defeated in the Revolutionary War. Miami war chief Little Turtle and other Native American leaders refused to agree that their rights to their lands were gone. From 1790 to 1795, Little Turtle led a group of Native American nations called the Miami Confederacy in raids and ambushes against Americans. President Washington sent several generals to battle the *confederacy*. General **Anthony Wayne** (see p. 124) resisted an attack by Little Turtle's forces at Fort Recovery. He then followed the Native Americans when they moved north. The Miami Confederacy was finally defeated at the Battle of Fallen Timbers, near present-day Toledo, Ohio. One year later, Native Americans from one dozen nations signed the Treaty of Greenville. This treaty gave the U.S. rights to what is now Ohio and part of Indiana.

Lord Dunmore's War

Military conflict in 1774. Virginia colonial governor John Dunmore conducted a survey of lands in Kentucky and Ohio. These lands had been granted to the **Shawnee** (see p. 45) in a treaty. The Shawnee killed all but one of the survey team. Massacres by both parties continued. Lord Dunmore sent an

Chief Logan's Lament

In response to incursions by white settlers in the Ohio Valley, and to the massacre of his family by whites, John Logan, a Cayuga-Mingo chief, joined in leading a military campaign against the settlers. The conflict became known as Lord Dunmore's War (1774), after the royal governor of Virginia. Defeated, Logan sent to Lord Dunmore the following defiant speech.

I appeal to any white man to say, if ever he entered Logan's cabin hungry, and he gave him not meat: if ever he came cold and naked, and he cloathed him not. During the course of the last long and bloody war Logan remained idle in his cabin, an advocate for peace. Such was my love for the whites, that my countrymen pointed as they passed, and said, "Logan is the friend of white man." I had even thought to have lived with you, but for the injuries of one man. Colonel Cresap, the last spring, in cold blood, and unprovoked, murdered all the relations of Logan, not even sparing my women and children. There runs not a drop of my blood in the veins of any living creature. This called on me for revenge. I have sought it: I have killed many: I have fully glutted my vengeance: for my country I rejoice at the beams of peace. But do not harbour a thought that mine is the joy of fear. Logan never felt fear. He will not turn on his heel to save his life. Who is there to mourn for Logan?—Not one.

Source: *Virginia Gazette.*

army to fight the Native Americans. The conflict ended in the Battle of Point Pleasant. The Native Americans were defeated, and a truce was signed in 1774.

Osceola *(ahs-ee-OHL-uh)*

Seminole (see p. 116) war leader. Osceola (1800–1838) rose to importance by opposing settlers who were moving into Florida. Andrew Jackson had invaded Florida during the First Seminole War. After he became president, he began to relocate Native Americans from the Southeast to lands west of the Mississippi River. Some Seminole, however, refused to leave Florida. They fought under Osceola's leadership. After winning a battle at the Withlacoochee *(with-luh-COO-chee)* River, Osceola attended a peace council with the Americans. He was immediately put in prison, where he died. The Second **Seminole War** (see p. 117)

Osceola.
(Library of Congress)

Red Eagle surrenders to General Andrew Jackson at Horseshoe Bend. (Library of Congress)

continued. The Seminole never surrendered, and many remained in Florida even after a third war in 1855–1858.

Red Bird

Winnebago (see p. 48) war chief. Red Bird (1790–1828) was a leader of the Winnebago Uprising. It was the result of Winnebago anger with lead miners, the imprisonment of Winnebago warriors, and abuse of Winnebago women by settlers. The uprising ended with Red Bird's surrender. He was imprisoned and died in 1828.

Red Eagle

Creek (see p. 29) leader. Raised in Alabama, Red Eagle (c. 1780–1882) was born William Weatherford. He was the son of a Scottish father and a Creek mother. The family allowed their sons to choose between the European and Native American lifestyles. Red Eagle became the leader of the Red Sticks. They were Creek who supported Tecumseh in **Tecumseh's Rebellion** (see p. 118). Red Eagle led the Red Sticks during the Creek War. In response to one attack, the U.S. army sent 3,500 troops under General **Andrew Jackson** (see p. 108) to fight the Red Sticks. Red Eagle surrendered to Jackson following the loss of a battle at Horseshoe Bend.

Red Jacket on Missionary Efforts

Seneca leader Red Jacket opposed Christian missionary efforts among his people. In 1805, he explained to some missionaries why he did not want to accept their religion. In so doing, he displayed the speaking skill for which he was renowned.

Brother!—Our seats were once large, and yours were very small. You have now become a great people, and we have scarcely a place left to spread our blankets. You have got our country, but are not satisfied. You want to force your religion upon us...Brother!—We do not understand these things. We are told that your religion was given to your forefathers, and has been handed down from father to son. We also have a religion which was given to our forefathers, and has been handed down to us their children. We worship that way. It teaches us to be thankful for all the favors we receive, to love each other, and to be united. We never quarrel about religion.

Brother!—The Great Spirit has made us all. But he has made a great difference between his white and red children. He has given us a different complexion and different customs. To you he has given the arts; to these he has not opened our eyes. We know these things to be true. Since he has made so great a difference between us in other things, why may we not conclude that he has given us a different religion, according to our understanding? The Great Spirit does right....He knows what is best for his children....We are satisfied....

Source: B. B. Thatcher, *Indian Biography*.

Red Jacket

Seneca leader. Red Jacket (c. 1750–1830) received his name from his involvement with the red-coated British during the **American Revolution** (see p. 99). After the war, he negotiated peace with the Americans. He later fought with them against the British in the **War of 1812** (see p. 123). Red Jacket was also well known for speaking out against the forced conversion of his people to Christianity. However, upon his death, missionaries took possession of his body and gave him a Christian burial.

Ridge, John

Cherokee (see p. 25) tribal leader. John Ridge (1803–1839) was educated in Connecticut and became well known as a Cherokee leader. He wrote for the *Cherokee Phoenix*, a Cherokee-language

John Ridge.
(Library of Congress)

newspaper. In 1835, Ridge, his father, his cousin Elias Boudinot, and 17 other Cherokee signed the Treaty of New Echota. This treaty gave Cherokee lands east of the Mississippi River to the U.S. government. The Cherokee Nation was later forced to move west.

Ross, John

John Ross.
(Library of Congress)

Cherokee (see p. 25) leader. The son of a Scottish father and a Scottish-Cherokee mother, John Ross (1790–1866) became involved in politics. He led Cherokee warriors with Andrew Jackson against the Creek in the Horseshoe Bend War. Ross was president of the Cherokee National Council and helped write the Cherokee Constitution. In 1828, he was elected chief of the Cherokee Nation. Ross opposed the 1835 Treaty of New Echota, which gave Cherokee lands to the U.S. government. He was the head of the United Cherokee until his death in 1866.

Sacajawea (*sack-uh-juh-WAY-uh*)

Shoshone (see p. 45) interpreter on the **Lewis and Clark expedition** (see p. 110). Sacajawea (ca. 1787–1812) was captured by a **Hidatsa** (see p. 34) raiding party when she was ten. She later became the wife of French fur trader Toussaint Charbonneau. Meriwether Lewis and William Clark met her when their expedition spent the winter with the **Mandan** (see p. 37) in present-day North Dakota. Lewis and Clark realized that Sacajawea could help them speak with other Native Americans. They hired Charbonneau to go with them only if Sacajawea would join him.

Sacajawea helped the expedition as it met other nations in several ways. She helped speak with the other nations for Lewis and Clark, and she reassured the other Native Americans that the expedition was peaceful. It is often thought she guided the expedition across the Rocky Mountains. This is not true. She did, however, point out landmarks to Lewis and Clark and introduce them to edible roots and plants. After the expedition, events in her life are unknown. It is believed that she died in 1812. There are now more statues of Sacajawea than of any other American woman.

Seminole

People of the Southeast **culture area** (see p. 30). The Seminole were originally members of the **Creek** (see p. 29) Confederacy.

This illustration appeared in a newspaper article aimed at winning support for the Seminole Wars. It shows Seminole warriors and the escaped African slaves that had joined them attacking white settlers. (Library of Congress)

They fled U.S. capture in the early 19th century. The Seminole settled in Florida and lived by fishing and hunting. They welcomed Native Americans from other nations and runaway enslaved Africans. The Seminole resisted removal from Florida in three wars with the U.S. called the **Seminole Wars** (see below). Following their surrender, they were sent to Oklahoma.

Seminole Wars

Wars (1817–1818; 1835–1842; 1855–1858) fought by the U.S. against the Seminole. The first began when **Andrew Jackson** (see p. 108) led an army into Florida. His goal was to punish **Seminole** (see p. 116) who were hiding runaway slaves.

The second war was an outcome of the Indian Removal Act of 1830. This law directed that all Native Americans in the Southeast be relocated west of the Mississippi River. While 3,000 Seminole were forced to leave Florida, others, led by **Osceola** (see p. 113), resisted the removal and fought against the Americans. The Americans finally withdrew their forces in 1842.

The third war began when government workers destroyed crops belonging to Seminole leader **Billy Bowlegs** (see Vol. 2, p. 22). The Seminole began to attack the settlers, surveyors, and trappers in the Everglades of Florida. The U.S. forces lost most of the attacks. The Seminole never signed a treaty, and many remained in Florida, where they still live today.

Sequoyah (*suh-KWOY-uh*)

Creator of the **Cherokee** (see p. 25) alphabet. Sequoyah (ca. 1776–1843) was the son of a colonial trader and a Cherokee

Sequoyah.
(Library of Congress)

woman. He never learned to speak or write English. However, he knew the English communicated by writing. He worked to turn the Cherokee spoken language into written characters. Sequoyah developed a kind of alphabet called a *syllabary*. His syllabary contained characters that represented syllables instead of letters. It had 85 characters. He called these "talking leaves." Sequoyah's daughter used the syllabary to record the speeches made at a Cherokee council. Sequoyah then entered the council and read the speeches from the record his daughter made. In this way, he showed the council how the syllabary worked. In a short time, thousands of Cherokee were learning to read and write using the syllabary. A newspaper, the *Cherokee Phoenix*, began publishing with columns in English and Cherokee. Sequoyah also translated much of the Bible into the new written language.

Tecumseh's Rebellion

Resistance led by the Shawnee (see p. 45) chief Tecumseh. Tecumseh's Rebellion began in 1809, when the Treaty of Fort Wayne was signed. William Henry Harrison (see p. 103), then governor of Indiana Territory, had tricked some minor chiefs into signing away millions of acres of Native American land. Tecumseh protested to Harrison, but the land was not returned. His followers wanted him to go to war. Tecumseh believed that if Native American nations would join together, they could protect their lands and preserve their ways of life. He traveled the country to try to unite Native American nations. While Tecumseh was traveling, Harrison ordered an attack on and burned a Shawnee village by the Tippecanoe (*tip-uh-cuh-NOO*) River. The attack led Tecumseh to join forces with the British in the War of 1812 (see p. 123).

Tecumseh.
(Library of Congress)

After helping the British capture Detroit, Tecumseh was made a brigadier general. As he and his warriors were protecting the British, they were attacked by Harrison's American forces. Tecumseh was killed. His death ended both his rebellion and his plan for a permanent homeland for all Native Americans.

Tenskwatawa *(ten-skwuh-TAH-wuh)*

Shawnee (see p. 45) prophet. Tenskwatawa (ca. 1768–ca. 1834) was the twin brother to the great Shawnee leader Tecumseh (see

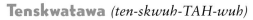

Tecumseh's Speech

Shawnee chief Tecumseh traveled around the country urging other Native American nations to join him in the war against the U.S. known as Tecumseh's Rebellion (1809–1813). In 1811, he spoke in the South to a council of Choctaw and Chickasaw, trying to convince them to join his alliance. In the passage below, he appealed to their memory of how white Americans had robbed other Indian nations of their lands.

But have we not courage enough remaining to defend our country and maintain our ancient independence? Will we calmly suffer the white intruders and tyrants to enslave us? Shall it be said of our race that we knew not how to [free] ourselves from the three most dreadful [disasters]—folly, inactivity, and cowardice? But what need is there to speak of the past? It speaks for itself and asks, Where today is the Pequot? Where the Narragansetts, the Mohawks, Pocanokets, and many other once powerful tribes of our race? They have vanished before the [greed] and oppression of the white men, as snow before a summer sun. In the vain hope of alone defending their ancient possessions, they have fallen in the wars with the white men. Look abroad over their once beautiful country, and what see you now? Naught but the ravages of the pale face destroyers meet our eyes. So it will be with you Choctaws and Chickasaws! Soon your mighty forest trees, under the shade of whose wide spreading branches you have played in infancy, sported in boyhood, and now rest your wearied limbs after the fatigue of the chase, will be cut down to fence in the land which the white intruders dare to call their own. Soon their broad roads will pass over the grave of your fathers, and the place of their rest will be blotted out forever. The [destruction] of our race is at hand unless we unite in one common cause against the common foe. Think not, brave Choctaws and Chickasaws, that you can remain passive and indifferent to the common danger, and thus escape the common fate. Your people, too, will soon be as falling leaves and scattering clouds before their blighting breath. You, too, will be driven away from your native land and ancient domains as leaves are driven before wintry storms.

Source: Tecumseh, *Speech to the Choctaw and Chickasaw*.

p. 118). Tenskwatawa preached a return to traditional Native American ways. He wanted all Native American nations to abandon European and colonial customs, including the practice of Christianity and the use of alcohol. Some warriors persuaded Tenskwatawa to attack the forces of **William Henry Harrison**

The Battle of Tippecanoe was a great defeat for the Shawnee. (Library of Congress)

(see p. 103). Harrison's army burned Tenskwatawa's village, Prophetstown. This defeat discouraged other nations that Tecumseh had hoped to bring together. Tenskwatawa continued to preach traditional Native American values until his death.

Tippecanoe, Battle of

Significant skirmish in **Tecumseh's Rebellion** (see p. 118). **Shawnee** (see p. 45) chief Tecumseh and his brother **Tenskwatawa** (see p. 118) founded Prophetstown. The village, also called Tippecanoe, was near the junction of the Wabash and Tippecanoe rivers in Indiana Territory. As settlers moved further onto Native American lands, Tecumseh tried to unite the Native American nations. His brother Tenskwatawa preached a return to old Indian ways.

William Henry Harrison (see p. 103), the governor of the territory, was alarmed by Tecumseh's efforts. He wanted to force the Shawnee into a war. Harrison accused the Shawnee of stealing some army horses. He then led a force of 1,000 to within a few miles of Prophetstown. Tecumseh did not want to go to war, but his brother was persuaded by some warriors to attack Harrison's forces. Harrison's men held their ground and Tenskwatawa withdrew. Prophetstown was left empty, and Harrison destroyed the village.

This became the Battle of Tippecanoe. It was important because it discouraged other nations from joining Tecumseh's

The map above shows the routes taken to Indian Territory by Native American nations of the Southeast during the 1830s. The Trail of Tears, as the Cherokee journey was called, took place in 1838 and 1839. The first nation to be removed was the Choctaw, who moved west also starting in 1831. The map shows the current borders of the U.S. states.

efforts to unite Native American nations. The battle made Harrison a national hero. He used it to promote himself during his successful campaign for president in 1840.

Trail of Tears

Name for the route taken by the **Cherokee** (see p. 25) during their removal from Georgia to Oklahoma (1838–1839). President **Andrew Jackson** (see p. 108) signed the Indian Removal Act of 1830. This act allowed the removal of Native Americans west across the Mississippi River. The **Choctaw** (see p. 27) were the first people to be moved under the act. The Cherokee sued the U.S. over the act. The Supreme Court ruled the law unconstitutional in *Worcester* v. *State of Georgia*. Jackson, however, ignored the ruling.

The Treaty of New Echota (*eh-COH-tuh*) was signed in 1835. By signing the treaty, a small group of Cherokee agreed to leave their homeland. Most other Cherokee ignored the treaty.

The Trail of Tears

From 1838 to 1839, the Cherokee were forced to move from Georgia to Oklahoma in a difficult journey that became known as the Trail of Tears. A white traveler from Maine saw them in December 1838 as they passed through Kentucky.

...We met several detachments in the southern part of Kentucky on the 4th, 5th, and 6th of December....The last detachment which we passed on the 7th embraced rising two thousand Indians with horses and mules in proportion. The forward part of the train we found just pitching their tents for the night, and notwithstanding some thirty or forty wagons were already stationed, we found the road literally filled with the procession for about three miles in length. The sick and feeble were carried in wagons—about as comfortable for traveling as a New England ox cart with a covering over it—a great many ride on horseback and multitudes go on foot—even aged females, apparently nearly ready to drop into the grave, were traveling with heavy burdens attached to the back—on the sometimes frozen ground, and sometimes muddy streets, with no covering for the feet except what nature had given them...We learned from the inhabitants on the road where the Indians passed, that they buried fourteen or fifteen at every stopping place, and they make a journey of ten miles per day only on average.

John Ehle, *Trail of Tears: The Rise and Fall of the Cherokee Nation.*

They believed the signers of the treaty had no right to give up Cherokee lands. In 1838, the next U.S. president, Martin Van Buren, sent troops into Georgia to round up Cherokee families. The Cherokee were forced to walk to camps in Tennessee and today's Oklahoma. Weather conditions, hunger, and disease killed some 4,000 of the 15,000 who made the journey. The Cherokee called their route "The Trail Where They Cried." The term "Trail of Tears" was later used to describe the relocation of all Native American peoples from the Southeast during the 1830s.

treaties

Legal agreements between two nations. Treaties between Native Americans and Britain or its colonies date from 1614. This was when Chief **Powhatan** (see p. 83) agreed to peace with English settlers at Jamestown. Most colonists were known for breaking treaties. However, there were exceptions. Pennsylvania colony founder **William Penn** (see p. 77) kept his word in agreements with the **Delaware** (see p. 30) Nation.

The first treaty between Native Americans and the U.S. government was signed at Fort Pitt, today's Pittsburgh, in 1778. It gave the Delaware the right to send representatives to Congress. In return, the Delaware would support the colonies. The terms of this treaty never happened. Over the next century, the U.S. Senate agreed to some 370 treaties with Native American nations. Treaties were made for a variety of reasons. Some were made to gain the support of one Native American nation against another. Most were made to obtain land for settlers. The U.S. Constitution gave the federal government the right to make Native American treaties. It said that Congress could "regulate Commerce...with the Indian tribes."

Treaties were frequently made in good faith. However, most were broken or ignored by the settlers who moved across the country.

The system of formal treaties ended in 1871. That year, Congress declared all future agreements with Native Americans would be decided by the president or by Congress. The government no longer felt it needed to make formal arrangements with native nations. The U.S. viewed Native Americans as people who no longer had any power or rights. In very recent years some of the rights of Native Americans under the old treaties have been acknowledged. For example, the Oneida, who lost lands in New York State, have now received federal support in their claims against the state government.

War of 1812

The second and final major conflict between the U.S. and Great Britain, lasting from 1812 to 1814. One cause of the war was the belief that the Native Americans and the British were united against the U.S. The U.S. and the Native American nations were battling over the loss of native lands. Many believed that the British were aiding Native American nations in these struggles. This belief was reinforced when American troops defeated a combined British and Native American force at the Battle of the Thames.

During the War of 1812, the British captured Washington, D.C. When the United States won several sea battles, the war came to an end. The Treaty of Ghent, signed in December 1814, officially ended the conflict.

Wayne, Anthony

Soldier known as "Mad" Anthony Wayne. Wayne (1745–1796) was a colonel in the American army in 1776. He negotiated treaties with the **Creek** (see p. 29) and **Cherokee** (see p. 25) in 1782–1783. In 1791, George Washington sent Wayne to stop a Native American rebellion in what is now Indiana. At the Battle of Fallen Timbers, Wayne attacked and destroyed the villages of the Native American rebels. This victory resulted in the Treaty of Greenville. The terms of the treaty gave the Native American lands of today's Ohio and much of Indiana to the United States.

Anthony Wayne.
(Library of Congress)

western exploration and trade

In the early 19th century, most of the regions in North America west of the Mississippi River remained as Native American lands. The Spanish had colonized scattered parts of the Southwest and California. They built missions in California and elsewhere to convert Native Americans to Catholicism. By the early 1800s, Spain's power had weakened. One cause was revolts among Native Americans, such as the Yuma Uprising along the California-Arizona border in 1781. By 1821, Mexico, Spain's largest colony in the Americas, had won its independence from Spain. Meanwhile, Missouri, on the west bank of the Mississippi, had been admitted to the U.S. as a state. In the 1830s, Texas, then part of Mexico, declared itself an independent republic. But most of the West remained the country of Native Americans. Some explorers and traders from the United States and Europe were beginning to discover the West.

In the Pacific Northwest, the Russians were exploring Alaska. Vitus Bering became the first European to sight Alaska. Russian fur traders began establishing trading posts. The Native Americans they met were not treated well. The Russians took the women as hostages and forced the men to trap furs. The Aleut (*al-OOT*) and the **Tlingit** (*TLIN-git*) (see p. 47) attacked and destroyed the Russian settlement of New Archangel. The

Russians eventually expanded their trading activities down the coast as far as California. There, they established Fort Ross just north of San Francisco.

By the end of the 18th century, Russia was not alone in the fur trade in the Pacific Northwest. Merchant ships from Spain, Britain, and the United States were also present. American trading posts included Astoria, Oregon. Astoria was a port settlement founded by John Jacob Astor. American explorers and traders were also coming by land. **Meriwether Lewis and William Clark** (see p. 110) explored the Louisiana Territory. Wagon caravans on the Santa Fe Trail to New Mexico and steamboats on the upper Missouri River carried traders to Native Americans. Beginning in the 1820s, fur trappers and traders, known as mountain men, were moving into the Rocky Mountains.

These and other explorers and traders were often the first European people encountered by western Native American nations. These pioneers found trails through the wilderness and

A Smallpox Victim

In 1837, a steamboat carrying supplies to a trading post in North Dakota brought a cargo of smallpox by mistake. The steamboat's crew, sick with the disease, passed it to the Mandan, Hidatsa, Assiniboine, Arikara, Sioux, and Blackfoot along the upper Missouri River. The illness spread like wildfire, killing at least 17,000 people. In this speech, one of the victims, a Mandan called The Four Bears, blamed white men for the disease that had disfigured and would soon kill him.

...I have never called a White Man a Dog, but today, I do pronounce them to be a set of Black hearted Dogs...I have been in Many Battles, and often Wounded, but the Wounds of My Enemies I exalt in...I do not fear Death, my friends. You know it, but to die with my face rotten, that even Wolves will shrink with horror at seeing Me....Listen well what I have to say, as it will be the last time you will hear Me. Think of your Wives, Children, Brothers, Sisters, Friends, and in fact all that you hold dear, are all Dead, or Dying, with their faces all rotten, caused by the dogs the whites, think of all that My friends, and rise all together and Not leave one of them alive. The 4 Bears will act his part.

Source: George Catlin, *Letters and Notes on the North American Indians*.

later served as scouts for European-American settlers. They were forerunners for the many settlers who would come later in the century.

Winnebago Uprising

The government had discouraged Native Americans from mining and selling lead. However, settlers continued to do so in present-day southwest Wisconsin. Tensions between settlers and the Winnebago (see p. 48) increased over the mining activities. In 1827, some Winnebago warriors attacked and killed settlers. In other events, Winnebago women were captured. Winnebago Chief Red Bird (see p. 114) organized a group to rescue the women. U.S. troops were sent to stop the activities of Red Bird's group. Other government officials met with peaceful Winnebago to keep them from siding with Red Bird. He surrendered and was imprisoned.

Glossary

adobe: the sun-dried brick made of clay used by Pueblo peoples of the Southwest for building.

annex: when referring to land or territory, to add or take the land of another people or nation.

anthropologist: a scientist who studies human beings, especially their physical and cultural habits, customs, and relationships.

Archaic: ancient; when referring to Native American history, the Archaic period lasted from 9000 to 1000 BCE.

archeologist: a scientist who excavates, or carefully digs out, objects that have been buried in the ground. Archeologists try to learn about the cultures of people from the past by studying the remains of the ancient objects that belonged to them.

band: the form of political organization customarily found among hunter-gatherers. Bands usually have no permanent leaders; decisions are based on building consensus. Leadership tends to be situational, arising for short periods of time.

Beringia: the land bridge that historians say attached modern-day Alaska to Asia, across the Bering Strait.

bounty: a reward or payment given by the government for killing or capturing a specific person or people. Bounties were often offered for the scalps of Native Americans.

clan: a tribal division, made up of people sharing a common ancestor.

confederacy: people, groups or nations united for a common purpose, such as the Iroquois Confederacy.

conquistador: a Spanish conqueror of Mexico, Peru, or other parts of 16th-century America.

council house: a special building used for important decision-making meetings.

disease: illness; because Native Americans and Europeans had been separated for thousands of years, they had developed different diseases. They also had differing abilities to fight them off. Many thousands of Native Americans died from diseases spread by Europeans, such as smallpox, typhus, and cholera.

earth lodge: the permanent den or hut of a Native American, made of sod.

encomienda: a Spanish word for the system developed during the 16th century for commissioning or granting by the king of Spain the slave labor of local native peoples to Spanish settlers.

epidemic: a contagious disease that becomes widespread throughout a community, making many people sick at the same time.

fluting: decorations or markings consisting of rounded grooves.

forage: to search for food or supplies.

Great Spirit: the chief god in the religion of many Native American nations.

igloo: a temporary Inuit house or hut, usually in the shape of a dome, built with blocks of snow or ice. Igloos were used during long expeditions, not as permanent houses.

irrigation: the system of watering by means of ditches or artificial channels or by sprinklers.

lean-to: a building with a sloping roof, in which the upper ends of the rafters rest against a tree or other support. In the case of a "double lean-to," one wall rested against the other for support.

longhouse: a communal house, shared by many families. Longhouses were common among the Iroquois.

mesa: a small flat plateau, common in the Southwest.

mestizo: the term for a person of mixed Spanish-Native American ancestry. Most people in Latin America today are mestizos.

migration: the act of moving from one place to another, especially to leave one's homeland to settle in another.

militia: an army composed of regular citizens instead of professional soldiers.

mosaic: the process of making pictures or designs with inlaid bits of stone, glass, or tile in mortar.

nomad: a member of a nation or tribe with no permanent home, who moves from place to place hunting and gathering food.

Paleolithic: the ancient period of prehistory that lasted from about 35,000 BCE to 9000 BCE.

patroonship: granting of a large estate by the Dutch king to Dutch settlers in colonial New Netherland.

pictograph: a picture or symbol representing an idea, often as an early form of writing.

Postarchaic: the period in ancient history that lasted from 1500 BCE to 1500 CE.

prairie: rolling grasslands, as in much of the lands between the Mississippi River and Rocky Mountains.

pueblo: a communal village built by many native peoples of the Southwest, made up of flat-roofed structures of stone or adobe, arranged in terraces. The word is also used to describe the nations that live in this style of village, such as the Hopi or Zuñi.

smallpox: a deadly disease that killed many Native Americans. In one incident, British soldiers purposely infected blankets with smallpox, and gave them as "gifts" to Native Americans.

syllabary: a set of written signs or characters, each representing a syllable.

totem pole: a pole carved and painted with totems, or sacred animals thought to be related to family members or ancestors. Totem poles were usually placed in front of the homes of members of Native American nations in the Northwest Coast region.

tribal status: a federal government designation. The U.S. government periodically reviews the state of Native American nations or tribes to decide if each of them has enough members to be recognized as a tribe. If a tribe does, then it continues to receive benefits and privileges of tribal status.

vigilante: a person who is not a member of an official law enforcement group that takes it upon him- or herself to enforce laws. Vigilantes often use violence to achieve their goals.

ward: someone who is under the control of a guardian. For instance, in the "trust relationship" between Native Americans on the reservations and the United States, Native American peoples were seen as childlike "wards" of the government, rather than as equals.

wickiup: a temporary style of house made of grass and brush, over a wood frame.

wigwam: a dome-shaped type of housing, made up of poles covered with sheets of bark or branches. Common to the Cherokee and other Southeast peoples.

World maker: A supernatural figure who is part of Native American stories of how the earth was created.

Resources

General Subjects

BOOKS

Aliki. *Corn Is Maize: The Gift of the Indians.* New York: Harper Collins, 1986.

Ancona, George. *Powwow.* San Diego, CA: Harcourt Brace Jovanovich, 1993.

Baquedano, Elizabeth. *Eyewitness: Aztec, Inca and Maya.* London and New York: DK Publishing, 2000.

Brown, Fern G. *American Indian Science: A New Look at Old Cultures.* New York: Twenty-First Century Books/Henry Holt and Co., 1997.

Caduto, Michael J., and Joseph Bruchac. *Keepers of the Earth: Native American Stories and Environmental Activities for Children.* Golden, CO: Fulcrum, 1988.

Erdoes, Richard. *The Rain Dance People: The Pueblo Indians, Their Past and Present.* New York: Alfred A. Knopf, 1976.

Fichter, George S. *American Indian Music and Musical Instruments.* New York: David McKay Co., 1978.

Gridley, Marion E. *American Indian Tribes.* New York: Dodd, Mead & Co., 1974.

Hirschfelder, Arlene B. *Happily May I Walk: American Indians and Alaska Natives Today.* New York: Scribner's, 1986.

Hofsinde, Robert (Gray-Wolf). *Indian Hunting.* New York: William Morrow and Company, 1962.

_____. *Indian Sign Language.* New York: William Morrow and Co., 1960.

Hoyt-Goldsmith, Diane. *Pueblo Storyteller.* New York: Holiday House, 1991.

Jacobson, Daniel. *Indians of North America.* New York: Franklin Watts, 1983.

Kavasch, E. Barrie, ed. *Native American Folklore, Activities and Foods.* Peterborough, NH: Cobblestone Publishing Inc., 1994.

La Pierre, Yvette. *Native American Rock Art: Messages from the Past.* Charlottesville, VA: Thomasson-Grant, Inc., 1994.

Liptak, Karen. *North American Indian Medicine People.* New York: Franklin Watts, 1990.

_____. *North American Indian Sign Language.* New York: Franklin Watts, 1992.

_____. *North American Indian Survival Skills.* New York: Franklin Watts, 1990.

_____. *North American Indian Tribal Chiefs.* New York: Franklin Watts, 1992.

Mather, Christine. *Native America: Arts, Traditions, and Celebrations.* New York: Clarkson Potter Publishers, 1990.

McLuhan, T. C. *Touch the Earth: A Self-Portrait of Indian Existence.* New York: Simon and Schuster, 1971.

Murdoch, David. *Eyewitness Books: North American Indian.* New York: Alfred A. Knopf in association with the American Museum of Natural History, 1995.

Niethammer, Carolyn. *American Indian Food and Lore.* New York: Collier Books, 1974.

Ortiz, Simon. *The People Shall Continue.* San Francisco: Children's Book Press, 1988.

Prentaz, Scott. *Native American Culture: Tribal Law.* Vero Beach, FL: Rourke Publications, Inc., 1994.

Roberts, Chris. *Powwow Country.* Helena, MT: American and World Geographic Publishing, 1992.

Sherrow, Victoria. *Native American Culture: Spiritual Life.* Vero Beach, FL: Rourke Publications, Inc., 1994.

Tannenbaum, Beulah, and Harold. Tannenbaum. *Science of the Early American Indians.* New York: Franklin Watts, 1988.

Whitney, Alex. *Sports and Games the Indians Gave Us.* New York: David McKay Co., Inc., 1977.

Wolfson, Evelyn. *From Abenaki to Zuni: A Dictionary of Native American Tribes.* Illus. by William Sauls Bock (Delaware). New York: Walker Publishing Co., Inc., 1988.

_____. *From the Earth to Beyond the Sky: Native American Medicine.* New York: Houghton Mifflin, 1993.

_____. *Growing Up Indian.* New York: Walker and Company, 1986.

Wood, Marian. *Ancient America: Cultural Atlas for Young People.* New York: Facts on File, 1990.

_____. *Myths and Civilization of the Native Americans.* New York: Peter Bedrick Books, 1998.

AUDIOCASETTES
The American Indian Oral History Collection. Ann Arbor, MI: Norman Ross Publishing Inc., 1977.

CD-ROM
Science through Native American Eyes. Kapaa, HI: Cradleboard Teaching Project, 1996.

VIDEO
Images of Indians (video series). Lethbridge, Alberta, Canada: Four Worlds Development Project, 1992.

Indians of North America (video series). Wynnewood, PA: Schlessinger Video Production, 1993–1994.

WEBSITES
American Indians: Apache, Blackfoot, Cherokee, Cheyenne, Lakota, and Pueblo: http://www.thewildwest.org/native_american/index.html

Edward S. Curtis's The North American Indian: Photographic Images: http://lcweb2.loc.gov/ammem/award98/ienhtml/tribes.html

Exploring Native Americans across the Curriculum: http://www.education-world.com/a_lesson/lesson038.shtml

The First Americans: http://www.germantown.k12.il.us/html/intro.html

The First Americans: Dineh, Muskogee, Tlingit, Lakota, Iroquois: http://www.u.arizona.edu/ic/kmartin/School/index.htm

First Nations Compact History: http://www.dickshovel.com/up.html

National Museum of the American Indian: http://www.nmai.si.edu/

Native American Website for Children: http://www.nhusd.k12.ca.us/ALVE/NativeAmerhome.html/nativeopeningpage.html

Native North America:
http://www.anthro.mankato.msus.edu/cultural/northamerica/index.shtml

NativeWeb: http://www.nativeweb.org/

WWW Virtual Library—American Indians: http://www.hanksville.org/NAresources/

History and Biography

(Before 1839)

BOOKS
Burt, Olive. *Sacajawea*. New York: Watts, 1978.

Dubowski, Cathy East. *The Story of Squanto, First Friend to the Pilgrims*. New York: Dell Yearling, 1990.

McCall, Barbara. *Native American Culture: The European Invasion*. Rourke Publications, Inc., 1994.

Ochoa, George. *The Fall of Quebec and the French and Indian War*. Englewood Cliffs, NJ: Silver Burdett, 1990.

Raphael, Elaine. *Sacajawea: The Journey West*. New York: Scholastic, 1994.

Sherrow, Victoria. *Political Leaders and Peacemakers*. Facts on File, 1994.

Voight, Virginia. *Sacajawea*. New York: Putnam, 1967.

Waldman, Carl. *Who Was Who in Native American History*. New York: Facts on File, 1990.

CD-ROM
People in the Past: Ancient Puebloan Farmers of Southwest Colorado. Delores, CO: Paradox Productions/Living Earth Studios, Inc., for the Anasazi Heritage Center, 1998.

VIDEO
Ancient Civilizations for Children: Ancient Inca. Wynnewood, PA: Schlessinger Media, 1998.

Ancient Civilizations for Children: Ancient Maya. Wynnewood, PA: Schlessinger Media, 1998.

Discovery Magazine: The Earliest Immigrants. New York: Discovery Channel, 2000.

Time-Life Lost Civilizations: Inca. Alexandria, VA: Time-Life Video and Television, 1995.

Time-Life Lost Civilizations: Maya. Alexandria, VA: Time-Life Video and Television, 1995.

The West: Empire upon the Trails (Episode Two). Washington, DC: The West Film Project and WETA, 2001.

The West: The People (Episode One). Washington, DC: The West Film Project and WETA, 2001.

WEBSITES
An American Hero: Tecumseh: http://www.jmu.edu/madison/tecumseh/index.htm

Black Hawk's War of 1832: http://lincoln.lib.niu.edu/blackhawk/

The California Missions: http://library.thinkquest.org/3615/

Fighting for a Continent: Newspaper Coverage of the English and French War for Control of North America, 1754-1760: http://earlyamerica.com/review/spring97/newspapers.html

French and Indian Wars:
http://www.bigchalk.com/cgi-bin/WebObjects/WOPortal.woa/Homework/Middle_School/
History/Wars_Conflicts_by_Region/Americas/French_Indian_War_27636.html

Grandpa Was an Indian Chief: Accounts of the Cherokee Trail of Tears:
http://rosecity.net/tears/trail/chief.html

National Portrait Gallery: Native Americans - Sequoyah:
http://www.npg.si.edu/col/native/index.htm

National Portrait Gallery: Native Americans - Tenskwatawa:
http://www.npg.si.edu/col/native/tensk.htm

Trail of Tears: North Georgia History: http://ngeorgia.com/history/nghisttt.html

World Book Online: French and Indian Wars: http://worldbook.bigchalk.com/210800.htm

Folklore, Fiction, and Poetry

BOOKS
Bierhorst, John. *The Woman Who Fell from the Sky: The Iroquois Story of Creation.* New York: Morrow, 1993.

Bruchac, Joseph. *Flying with the Eagle, Racing the Great Bear: Stories from Native North America.* BridgeWater Books, 1993.

Cannon, A. E. *The Shadow Brothers*. New York: Delacorte Press, 1990.

Cohlene, Terri. *Clamshell Boy: A Makah Legend*. Mahwah, NJ: Troll, 1991.

Dorris, Michael. *Morning Girl*. New York: Hyperion, 1992.

Esbensen, Barbara. *The Star Maiden: An Ojibway Tale*. Boston: Little, Brown, 1988.

Goble, Paul. *Brave Eagle's Account of the Fetterman Fight*. Lincoln: University of Nebraska Press (Bison Books), 1992.

_____. *Iktomi and the Ducks*. New York: Orchard Books, 1990.

Green, Richard G. (Mohawk). *A Wundoa Book: "I'm Number One."* Sacramento, CA: Ricara Features, 1980, 1981, 1982, 1983.

Greene, Jacqueline Dembar. *Manabozho's Gifts: Three Chippewa Tales*. Boston: Houghton Mifflin, 1994.

Lavitt, Edward, McDowell and Robert E. *Nihancan's Feast of Beaver: Animal Tales of the North American Indians*. Santa Fe, NM: Museum of New Mexico Press, 1990.

Mayo, Gretchen Will. *Earthmaker's Tales: North American Indian Stories about Earth Happenings*. New York: Walker Publishing Company, 1989.

_____. *Star Tales: North American Indian Stories about the Stars*. New York: Walker Publishing Company, 1987.

Medicine Story (Manitonquat). *The Children of the Morning Light: Wampanoag Tales*. New York: Macmillan, 1994.

Osofsky, Audrey. *Dreamcatcher*. New York: Orchard Books, 1992.

Robinson, Margaret A. *A Woman of Her Tribe*. New York: Scribner's, 1990.

San Souci, Robert. *Sootface: An Ojibwa Cinderella Story*. Illus. by Daniel San Souci. New York: Delacorte, 1994.

Sneve, Virginia Driving Hawk, ed. *Dancing Teepees: Poems of American Indian Youth*. New York: Holiday House, 1989.

Two Bulls, Marty Grant (Sioux). *Ptebloka: Tails from the Buffalo*. Vermillion, SD: Dakota Books, 1991.

Viola, Herman, general ed. *American Indian Stories*. Milwaukee: Raintree Publishers, 1990.

Selected Bibliography

Billard, Jules B., ed. *The World of the American Indian*. Washington, DC: National Geographic Society, 1974.

Brown, Dee. *Bury My Heart at Wounded Knee: An Indian History of the American West*. New York: Henry Holt & Co., 2001.

Capps, Benjamin. *The Great Chiefs*. Alexandria, VA: Time-Life Books, 1975.

Catlin, George. *Letters and Notes on the Manners, Customs, and Conditions of North American Indians*. New York: Dover Publications, 1985.

Collins, Richard, ed. *The Native Americans: The Indiginous People of North America*. New York: Smithmark Publishers, 1991.

Jhoda, Gloria. *Trail of Tears*. San Antonio, TX: Wings Press, 1995.

Josephy Jr., Alvin. *500 Nations: An Illustrated History of North American Indians*. New York: Alfred A. Knopf, 1994.

Kopper, Philip. *The Smithsonian Book of North American Indians Before the Coming of the Europeans*. Washington, DC: Smithsonian Books, 1986.

Lavender, David. *The Great West*. Boston: Houghton Mifflin Company, 1987.

Matthiessen, Peter. *In the Spirit of Crazy Horse*. New York: Penguin USA, 1992.

Nabokov, Peter. *Native American Testimony: A Chronicle of Indian-White Relations from Prophecy to the Present, 1492–2000*. New York: Penguin USA, 1999.

Smith, Carter. *The Explorers and Settlers: A Sourcebook on Colonial America*. Brookfield, CT: Millbrook Press, 1991.

Tanner, Helen Hornbeck. *The Settling of North America: The Atlas of the Great Migrations Into North America from the Ice Age to the Present*. New York: Macmillan USA, 1995.

Taylor, Colin F. *Native American Arts and Crafts*. London: Salamander Books, 1995.

Waldman, Carl. *Who Was Who in Native American History*. New York: Facts on File, 1990.

Ward, Geoffrey. *The West: An Illustrated History*. Boston: Little Brown and Company, 1996.

Index

Note: The index below contains entries for both volumes of the Student Almanac of Native American History. *The boldfaced number 1 refers to pages in the first volume. The boldfaced number 2 refers to pages in the second volume.*